The Most Hated Woman : The True Story of Valmae Fay Beck

Irene Cochrane

Published by Trellis Publishing, 2021.

THE MOST HATED WOMAN : THE TRUE STORY OF VALMAE FAY BECK

First edition. July 4, 2021.

Copyright © 2021 Irene Cochrane.

ISBN: 979-8224234806

Written by Irene Cochrane.

THE MOST HATED WOMAN

THE TRUE STORY OF VALMAE FAY BECK

RENE COLTRANE

Valmae Fay Beck had been sentenced to life in prison for the 1987 murder of 12-year-old Sian Kingi in Noosa, Queensland when she was taken to hospital on May 5th for a heart surgery. Once in hospital, police camped in the hospital in the hopes that Beck would reveal more information about her former husband's criminal actions and allow police to close some cold cases. However, Beck died at 6.15 p.m. on May 27, 2008, and never revealed anything else.

Beck was regarded as Queensland's most hated woman, and some rejoiced when she finally passed away. In the three weeks she was in hospital, she was apparently semi-conscious, in an incoherent state, and not responding to any verbal stimulus. Beck's health issues started after she was moved to Townsville Correctional Centre from Brisbane. In the jail, she was given a kitchen job, and her weight ballooned to 308 pounds. This put a great strain on her body, and she never bothered to remedy the situation.

Some say that this was Beck's way of repenting for her previous crimes.

Valmae Beck and Barrie Watts

Valmae Beck was a plumpish, pug-faced woman, and she did not consider herself a beauty. Because of this, she spent her time looking for love, and would always unquestionably follow her partner's wishes just to make sure that she was not left alone. In 1983, she met Barrie Watts, a man who was significantly younger than her, in Perth, Western Australia. At the time, Beck had already been married twice before and was a mother to six children.

Beck's relationship with Watts was far from ideal, but Beck had very little opinion of her own worth that she was just grateful for the attention. The two would argue about the tiniest of things, and Watts would always utter vile things about Beck to tear her down. In December 1986, these two unlikely partners finally tied the knot. Watts' treatment of Beck had completely broken her will, and she always went ahead with Watts' directives no matter how absurd they were.

Watts' mistreatment of Beck was not the only flaw in the relationship. Watts had a propensity for lusting after women who were not his wife. He never made any effort to conceal his roving eye, and this further fuelled Beck's belief that her much younger husband would soon leave her. As she kept thinking these thoughts, she made a vow that she would do anything to keep him with her. This meant carrying out his every demand, no matter how inhuman.

In their home was further evidence of Watts' specific type of woman. There were a number of pornographic videos in the home, which Watts would watch constantly. His favorite type of pornography featured very young women, especially those that looked like they were barely teenagers. He made no effort to conceal these tapes, and Beck would almost always catch him watching them. The tapes were a source of constant pain to Beck, who couldn't understand why her husband would not be satisfied with just her.

Human beings are never satisfied with one thing for too long. Soon enough, we begin seeking a bigger thrill. Watts was no exception. He started telling his wife about his depraved fantasies, which involved sleeping with a younger woman. He kept repeating his fantasy, and it soon became the biggest bone of contention in their household. The entire time, Beck was unwilling to let go of her depraved husband, and as with everything else, he managed to wear her down on this topic too. Watts changed his story to fit his wife's needs. He expressed to Beck that once he slept with one final woman, he would be over his fantasy and would be faithful only to her. Beck bought into the story, and even accepted to help him find the perfect woman to fulfill his fantasy.

Beck never revealed where her children were at the time, or even if Watts had tried out any of his fantasies with her daughters.

October – 11th November 1987

In early October, Watts and Beck decided to take a trip to Queensland. The two never revealed what the purpose of their trip had been. However, police speculated that Watts had finally decided that it was time to fulfill his fantasies, and that he wanted to be as far away from home as possible, to avoid being recognized. The couple got into their white 1973 HQ Holden station wagon and drove towards Queensland, passing through Melbourne. They found a house in Lowood, a town 31 miles from Brisbane. They rented the house and settled in soon after.

The two then set out and visited a couple of beaches, and whatever else they were up to was pretty much kept a secret. However, things took a different turn in November. Watts started becoming restless, and was more vocal about his sexual fantasy than before. He had left his pornography videos back in Western Australia, and was getting more and more agitated as time went by. The police have long suspected that much more went on in October, but there has been no proof of nefarious activity committed by the couple prior to November 10, 1987.

November 10th 1987 was a surprisingly busy day for Beck and Watts, as they finally set into motion their plan of getting Watts a younger woman to rape so that he could finally become absolutely faithful to Beck. They drove their Holden station wagon to the Ipswich General Hospital and staked out the hospital, looking for an opportunity to nab their victim.

The first attempt was over pretty much as soon as it began. A young nurse walked out of the hospital and walked to her car. Beck and Watts scanned the parking lot and confirmed that there were no witnesses present. Watts got out of the station wagon and quickly made his way to the nurse's car. He rapped on her window, immediately startling her. She took a quick glance at the skinny man and locked all her doors. She then started up her car and drove off. She did not report this incident to the police until after another incident had been reported.

Beck went back into the station wagon and decided to make another try. He was not going to give up on his mission that easily. Whether or not Beck was opposed to this idea is unknown. Later in the same night, Watts got the break he was waiting for, and this time he changed tactics. A young nurse had just left the hospital and was walking to her car. Beck drove the station wagon closer to the nurse's car, and Beck got out. He knocked on the woman's window and she looked up. He had a map in his hand and motioned for her to roll her window down. She complied. Watts then asked her to point out the direction to a location on the map since he was lost. The nurse looked over into the station wagon and saw Beck at the steering wheel. This gave her a sense of security. The nurse got out of her car and proceeded to show Watts directions on the map. As she was talking, she realized that Watts kept moving closer and closer, and at some point he was pressed up tight against her shoulder.

The nurse started feeling extremely uncomfortable, and glanced over into the back seat of the station wagon. Her eyes quickly noted the hessian bags and ropes in the back seat. She felt a churning in the pit of her stomach, and the nervousness she was feeling quickly turned into downright fear. Just as she was trying to figure out her next move, she got her lucky chance. A colleague stepped out of the hospital and started walking across the parking lot towards the cars. Beck immediately shifted his focus to the man, and the nurse saw her chance. She quickly hopped into her car, locked the doors and drove off. She also did not immediately report the incident to the police. However, she mentally noted the station wagon's number plate as LLF 429. She had inadvertently logged an important clue that would be vital for the investigation that was to come later. After their second unsuccessful attempt, Beck and Watts decided to call it quits. They left the hospital area and headed back to Lowood. However, this was just the beginning of their crime spree.

On 11th November 1987, Beck and Watts decided to give their plan another go. This time, Beck would be a more active participant. At 5.30 p.m., a retail assistant called Cheryl finished her shift at Target and decided to make her way home. It was after hours and the normally busy parking lot was nearly empty. She walked to her car and made her way to the parking lot's exit. Just as she was about to exit into the road, she came across a frumpy looking woman flagging her down, seemingly asking for directions. Cheryl slowed down and engaged the woman. As they were talking, a skinny man jumped out of nowhere brandishing a knife.

Cheryl started screaming for help and an altercation ensued. In the attack, Watts managed to cut his hand and left bloody fingerprints on one of the windows of Cheryl's car. Her screams quickly drew out a crowd of witnesses who saw the man and woman drive off in a white Holden station wagon. The attack left Cheryl visibly shaken. Nevertheless, she drove straight to a police station to report the incident. The detective who caught the case was 1st Class Constable Graham Hall of the Ipswich CIB. He noted Cheryl's description of the suspects and her car was processed by the evidence technicians.

Constable Hall went to the shopping center to interview witnesses. One person provided the detective with the number plate of the station wagon; LLE 439. At the time, nobody knew that this plate number was wrong. Constable Hall quickly chased down this lead. However, by 7 p.m., the number plate was linked to a Toyota Corolla in a nearby country town. The car was quickly cleared. Hall wasn't about to let this case off easily, so he set up a small newspaper article that described the incident and the car the suspects escaped in. Two days later, the second victim from the 10th November attack called into the station. She told police that the number plate of the car they were looking for was LLF 429. This still managed to make finding the car difficult. Constable Hall assigned one staffer the task of checking up all the combinations of the three plate numbers to see if they could find a match of a Holden station wagon. This proved to be the same as finding a needle in a haystack. The case went cold soon after, and Beck and Watts were not caught.

November 27, 1987

Elizabeth Young and Bill Wallace had been at the Castaways Creek Beach on the afternoon of November 27th 1987. At around 4 p.m., the two walked back to the Castaways Beach parking lot towards Wallace's four-wheel drive. Having had things stolen from his car before, Wallace was always on high alert whenever he was out. As the two made it to the parking lot, they immediately noticed a skinny disheveled man hovering in the parking lot. Wallace immediately got suspicious and kept his eye on the man. The disheveled man was none other than 35-year-old Barrie Watts. When he noticed the two staring at him, Watts went back to his car, the Holden station wagon, and drove off. Wallace immediately got into his car and followed the station wagon, noting down the plates; LLE 429. Little did he know that this would be the key to solving one of the most brutal murders in Noosa County's history.

Beck and Watts had spent that day visiting the beaches of Noosa Heads, and Castaway Creek was just one of the locations they had stopped at. At around 3.30 p.m., the two noticed the Noosa schoolchildren on the street after school was let out. Watts had spent the day drinking, and promptly told Beck that the day had finally arrived. He was going to make his wish come true. The run in with Wallace did nothing to dampen Watts' plans as he left the beach area and headed to the Pinaroo Park, where they scoped out the area for their next victim.

Watts was looking for a specific victim at this point in time. He wanted a girl who was barely 13, flat chested and a virgin. They sat at the park's parking area and watched for the person who would fit that description and bring Watts' search to an end. All the ones they noticed were accompanied by adults or friends, and Beck began getting impatient. Fifteen minutes after they got to the park, Beck and Watts started arguing about Watts' fantasy once more. Beck was getting tired of waiting when Watts suddenly told her, "There's a girl coming on a bike. Stop her. Talk to her."

12-year-old Sian Kingi had just left a hot bread shop at Noosa Junction. She had been shopping with her mother when she told her that she would meet her at home. Sian then hopped on her bike and started riding towards the park. Their home was less than a mile away, and Lynda Kingi was not worried about anything happening to her daughter. She watched her daughter—dressed in her uniform, white joggers, and pink socks – ride off in her 10-speed yellow girl's Repco racing bike. With her beautiful blue eyes, pretty face and tanned skin, Sian was Watts' dream come true, however twisted his fantasies were.

Ever the dutiful wife, Beck quickly followed her husband's directive. With her unassuming look and frumpish stature, the girl did not register any warning bells when Beck asked her to help find her dog. Beck told Sian that she had lost a little white poodle with a pink bowtie. When asked whether she had seen it, Sian responded that she had not. As Beck continued to distract the little girl, Watts crept up behind her and slammed a cloth over Sian's mouth, effectively making sure that her screams would not be heard. He then dragged Sian into the back seat of the station wagon. Beck indeed did have a dog with her on that day; it just wasn't a white poodle. Beck's blue heeler got excited as the commotion unfolded, jumped out of the car, and started barking. Beck quickly chased down the dog and brought it back to the car and quickly drove off. Sian's bike was left at the scene of the crime. The abduction took 30 seconds to execute, and no one was looking in the right direction at the time.

When Lynda Kingi got home at 4.45 p.m., she did not find her daughter at home. She was not worried and just assumed that her daughter had met her friends along the way and stopped to talk to them. Sian was a popular girl, and many described her as a happy and gentle soul. She was liked by many, and in the small town of Noosa Heads, she was one of the perfect citizens. Lynda set about her tasks for the evening, knowing that her daughter would walk into the home at any time before the dark settled. After all, nothing bad had ever happened to their little children in Noosa.

Sian was in the back of Watts' car, gagged and bound with glossy brown masking tape. The car was speeding down Tinbeerwah Mountain State Forest, 9 miles west of Tewantin. Watts took over driving the car, entered a forestry road, and parked just a few meters off the road. He left the car lights on, and told Beck to remove the gag from Sian's mouth. Beck took a pair of scissors and went into action. She carefully cut the tape, and made sure that Sian's hair was left untouched. She then started cutting Sian's underpants, just as she had been instructed by her husband. Sian never shed even a single tear as this was happening.

At 6 p.m., Sian's day took a horribly brutal turn. According to Beck's confession to police, Watts had laid a bedspread on the grass and took Sian to it. Beck had gone to the car and stayed there watching Watts committing the indecent acts on Sian. Watts forced Sian to perform acts of fondling, kissing, and touching before finally raping the little girl. This one hour ordeal was apparently exactly what Watts had been craving all along. After he was done, he told Sian, "It's all finished now, it's all over." Watts then told Sian to put her dress back on. He then tied her ankles with rope, bound her hands, and gagged her with tape. He turned her over so that she lay on her stomach, took Beck's belt and tied it around Sian's neck. He then placed one knee on Sian's back and started tightening the belt. During the entire ordeal, Sian had not uttered a word, had not cried, and yet had been visibly frightened. Her only words to Watts were, "you're hurting me," as he tightened the belt.

Beck stated that her dog started acting up again and she went to tie it to the back of the car. When she turned around, she found that Watts had turned over Sian's body and was stabbing her in the chest and throat. He then dragged her a few meters off the creek bank and dumped her into the bush. The two got into the station wagon and drove towards the highway. As they passed Six Mile Creek, between Tewantin and Cooroy, Watts threw a bundled up bedspread into the creek. In it were the knife, rope, belt, and tape used in the brutal murder. Beck started crying, and Watts promised her that everything would be okay. As they drove towards Lowood, they passed by Brisbane and bought milk and cat food. They arrived at the house at around 10 p.m., and Beck put their filthy clothes in the wash.

At around 8.15 p.m. that night, Lynda Kingi had spent hours frantically calling everyone she knew inquiring about her daughter. When her husband walked into the house, the two went out to look for their daughter, retracing Sian's path home. At the Pinaroo Park, they found their daughter's bike right where it had fallen. They loaded the bike onto their vehicle and headed to the police station. They walked in at 8.40 p.m. and found Detective-Sergeant Bob Atkinson on duty. Atkinson was the second of the two senior detectives in the Noosa police department. The three drove to the park where Sian's bike was found. Atkinson immediately feared the worst, and took quick actions to kick off the investigation.

At 11.05 p.m., the Sunshine Coast Daily night desk received a call from detective Atkinson, requesting that they run Sian's disappearance in their Saturday paper. They complied, and added a small piece with Sian's photo on it. At 5 a.m. on Saturday morning, the police began their search for Sian, and Atkinson log officially listed her as a missing person. That same morning, Watts woke up early in the morning to wash the car both inside and out in a bid to get rid of Sian's hairs. He then went back to the house and read the article about Sian's disappearance. That afternoon, when Beck returned from shopping,

Watts called her upstairs and told her about the television news piece about Sian's disappearance. When Beck asked him if he was paranoid, he stated that he was okay, but glad that Beck was by his side. The couple then went ahead and had sex.

On Sunday afternoon, Senior Sergeant Neil Magnussen, officer in charge of Sunshine Coast CIB, called Brisbane Homicide and asked for reinforcement. That same Sunday, Beck and Watts heard the radio bulletin that described Sian's abductors. Their hair color was mentioned, and the two spent the afternoon dying their hair. Beck became a blonde, changing her once burgundy hair. She then gave Watts a haircut and dyed his sun-bleached hair dark brown.

Senior Sergeant Bob Dallow gathered a dozen homicide detectives, and together with Magnussen, set up a murder room in the Noosa police station upon arrival at the station on Monday. The Noosa Heads community was appalled by the crime, and the 1,500 citizens quickly started contributing any information they had. The 20 detectives in the murder room were quickly overwhelmed by the tips that flooded into the office.

The police quickly realized that the callers made numerous references to a white 1973 Holden station wagon. While other descriptions were different, the model remained the same. They decided to start looking for the vehicle. In Queensland alone, there existed 10,000 white Holden station wagons. The police had their work cut out for them. However, they caught a break after Elizabeth Young walked into the Noosa station and recounted the encounter with Watts the previous Friday. Senior Constable Alan Bourke called Bill Wallace and asked him to stop by the station the next day. On Monday morning, the detectives had the number plate of Queensland's most sought after Holden station wagon. Bourke ran a check on the plates and found the address registered under it. On Tuesday, he called Watts' adoptive father, Roland Watts, who confirmed that his son and wife indeed had the station wagon, and that they had traveled to Queensland.

On Wednesday December 2nd, 1987, 18-year-old Neil Clarke was walking home through the State Forest when he smelled a strange odor. He thought nothing of it at the time and proceeded home. Later that night, he remembered the coverage of Sian's disappearance and realized that the smell might have been of the body. He called the police station at 9.33 a.m. the next morning after going back to the scene and confirming that it was a body. Atkinson picked the call. The murder room fell silent once they saw Atkinson's face change. Sian's body was found at the bank of a shallow sandy creek, her dress pulled up above her waist. Her nylon green backpack was tossed about 10 meters away, and her pants lay nearby. The pathologist found 12 stab wounds on her chest, with three stabs having pierced the heart. There were two massive cuts to her throat, and one had completely cut through the spine.

The search for the Holden wagon started yielding results when several people recalled seeing the said car parked in Lowood. When the police revealed that the body had been found, Beck and Watts quickly started packing up in preparation to flee the town. That day, Colin Harm was installing a telephone line in Lowood when he noticed the station wagon. He made a mental note of the number plate, which started with LLE, because he wanted to buy the same car model. Senior Constable John Stehr was driving in Lowood when he noticed a parked white Holden station wagon in his rearview mirror. He noted the plates, starting with LLE, because it was a foreign plate in the area. At the time, Bourke had called up to Perth requesting for a photo of Watts and Beck. However, the description he gave did not match Valmae Beck, but rather Valmae Forte.

Over the weekend of December 5th and 6th, the photos of the two, Beck and Watts, was finally sent to Bourke. They composed a bulletin and sent it to every law enforcement office in Australia, hoping that they would be picked up. This proved to be the police's best decision.

On Tuesday 9th December, the photos were rolled out. Stehr and Harm both called into the station, leading police to the house in Lowood. Neighbors picked out Beck and Watts from a lineup, and police went to the house. When they later went to the real estate agency's office, they found Watts' and Beck's signatures on the lease, and the agent showed them a money order that the couple had sent after fleeing on 4th December. It was sent from The Entrance, a holiday resort in New South Wales.

The Noosa police alerted the New South Wales police about the lead in the case, and in 10 hours, undercover agents were sent to The Entrance. Atkinson and Magnussen flew to Sydney and then headed straight to The Entrance. On Saturday December 12, 1987, an undercover agent spotted the Holden station wagon leaving The Entrance and tailed it. He called for backup and a team was sent, heavily armed because Watts was wanted for armed robbery back in Western Australia. The raid team obtained a key and at 5 p.m., made their way into the ground floor suite that the couple was staying in. The two seemed surprised at the sight of the cops, but they were not overly alarmed. All they wanted to know is why they were being arrested, since they had open warrants in Western Australia.

WHEN GIRLS NEXT DOOR KILL : THE TRUE STORY OF CINDY COLLIER & SHIRLEY WOLF

IRIS OWEN

"Today, Cindy and I ran away and killed an old lady. It was lots of fun" -
Shirley Wolf's journal, June 14th, 1983.

Shirley Wolf and Cindy Collier met in a juvenile detention center and had known each other for only a few hours when they decided to escape and randomly kill a stranger.

They would go to a senior condominium center in Auburn, California where they would seek an elderly victim.

They would find one in the eighty-five-year-old Anna Brackett. They entered her home under the ruse that they needed to use the phone to call their parents.

The girls would brutally murder the elderly woman in a crime so shocking that deputy sheriffs were initially in denial that two young girls would commit such a crime.

But how did they get to the point mentally where they could commit such a horrid act? This is the story of how they got there.

EARLY LIFE

Cindy Collier wasn't the nice girl next door. Her entire body language spoke of rage and hostility. By the age of twelve, she was a regular at the juvenile hall where she would routinely assaulting staff and inmate alike.

Incorrigible, she had been arrested for burglary, theft and drug possession.

Because of her age, Cindy was often spared jail time and was sentenced to community service. She would most often be sent to pick up litter on highways but the punishment wasn't enough to deter her from a life of crime.

"She was a smart ass towards everyone," former classmate Mike Fluty said.

No one was spared her rage. At fourteen years old, she had no problem harassing adults as well, randomly accosting people on the street.

"What are you looking at?" she asked a woman walking by as she smoked a cigarette. "You think you're better than me?"

She would then raise her fist to the woman and force her to run away. "Oooh!" Cindy taunted. "Ooooh! Come on, you want some?"

"Cindy liked to intimidate," forensic psychologist Paula Orange said. "She had learned it was better to be a predator than the prey very early on in life. Her early childhood would shape the monster she would become."

Cindy's parents divorced when she was one year old. Her mother would remarry but that would end in divorce as well. She would take care of Cindy and her three sons during the day and go to a waitress job at night.

Cindy stated that she had been raped by an undisclosed family member and by another man who threw her down a flight of stairs after he finished with her.

"Her mother reportedly had different children all by different men," Orange said. "Cindy was molested by one of her mother's endless string of men that she brought into the home."

Cindy would talk about her "rotten" childhood and describe being "raped a few times." She tried to commit suicide on several occasions but that only brought her more frustrations. So instead of harming herself, she decided she would harm others.

"I want them to pay," she said.

By the time she entered Chana High in Auburn, California, Cindy had a well-established reputation of someone who should be feared. Using physical intimidation, she would randomly choose a girl she didn't like and the bullying would begin. She would push and yell, getting in their face. Her victims would be spared no quarter, on one occasion, Cindy ripped the blouse of a girl and forced her to run down the street topless.

"She was a trained bully," Orange said. "She knew exactly how to push the buttons of her victims, strip them of their dignity. It was done to her at home so it was easy for her to pass along the abuse."

Cindy was a menacing presence on campus to the other petite girls. At 5'9" and 140 pounds, she could beat up any girl in the school. She had a strong jawline and broad shoulders but it was her eyes that set her apart from the average bully. Eyes that pierced through her victims and gave them an implicit message.

I want to kill you.

Cindy's crimes would not be limited to physical assaults. She would grab and take whatever she wanted. She would go into liquor stores, stuff food into her pockets and leave. She would go into malls and steal cassette tapes at the record store. After a few months, she graduated to stealing a car. This would land her in a juvenile detention center where she would be a kindred spirit unlike any other she had met before.

LIKE LOOKING INTO A MIRROR

Like Cindy, Shirley Wolf had been the victim of sexual abuse. Her father, Louis Wolf, would rape her. But the abuse didn't stop with just her father. She was a molested by her paternal grandfather and uncle as well.

An observant kindergarten teacher noticed the odd behavior of Shirley and recommended that she get psychiatric help to no avail.

Shirley didn't know where else to turn as she would be abused by all of the men in her life. At the age of six years old, she had run away for the first time. The streets were too rough for her, however, and she was scared back home by the dark characters of Brooklyn.

A lost little girl with nowhere else to go but the house where she was abused.

Her father, Louis, worked as a carpenter but suffered an accident that forced him to take disability. He would remain at home and begin bossing his children around. Then it turned to the sexual abuse of his daughter, Shirley.

When Shirley was around six, the family would move from the east coast to Placerville, California so Louis could be closer to his own family.

Louis Wolf would send Shirley's mother Katherine on an errand to get some groceries one morning. He then locked Shirley's three younger brothers out of the house and turned his attention to Shirley.

He cornered her in the bathroom and raped her.

Shirley would never forgive her father for what he did to her.

Louis would rape his daughter sometimes as much as three times per day. By the time she reached puberty, he put her on birth control.

Shirley never told her mother because she didn't want to break up the family.

Louis would tell Shirley to not tell her mother what he had done. Shirley obliged only because she was afraid how badly the news would hurt her mother.

Eventually, however, the abuse became so intolerable that she told her mother.

Her mother suspected it all along. She then went to the authorities.

Louis would deny that he molested Shirley but plead guilty to reduced charges which brought his sentencing down to a mere one-hundred days.

Louis was told that if he fought the charges, he would be facing fifty years. So he took the three months.

Shirley would then be removed from the home which was her worst fear. She would be bounced from foster home to foster home where she told of feeling "like a stranger."

"You get to the point where you're pushed in a corner and I just came back fighting," Shirley said. "I want to go home. I forgive my father and I try to forget it. He's apologized to me, my family and to God."

A MATCH TO A FLAME

It would be only fitting that the first time the girls would meet, it would be under the guise of violence.

At the detention center, Shirley was being beaten to a pulp by a fellow inmate in the hallway. As per usual, no guards were around. But Cindy stood her ground against the bigger girl, to no avail.

The girl threw her against the wall, punched her in the stomach and twisted her arm.

"Who are you?" Cindy asked as she came upon the two girls fighting.

"Shirley Wolf."

"I like you, Shirley Wolf."

And with that, Cindy got her opponent into a full nelson, easily overpowering Shirley's tormentor.

"Let her have it," Cindy said.

Shirley didn't hesitate. She began pummeling the girl, all of the rage of being abused all of her life came forth as she gave the girl a beat-down.

Cindy threw the girl to the ground and the two laughed as she moaned in pain.

"Later loser," Shirley sniffed.

Cindy laughed. The girl had spunk and they spent the next couple of hours exchanging their life stories.

For some reason, Cindy did not feel hatred toward Shirley. She felt like they had an unspoken bond but she didn't know why.

The truth was, they were both ticking time bombs.

"I think it was an unfortunate chemistry between the two girls," Shirley's defense attorney Thomas Condit said. "I think it also had to do with finding a new friend and wanting to show that she was capable of doing anything that the friend was."

Shirley was the opposite of Cindy in one regard, however, as she did not have Cindy's assurance. Shirley felt "hopeless and helpless" as she talked about running away from the detention center. She talked about this as if it were an impossibility, a faraway dream.

But Cindy felt otherwise. She behaved as if she knew all the answers.

"I can get us out of here," Cindy said with total assurance.

"You can?"

"Sure. I do it all the time. But we're going to need a car. This place where I used to live as all kinds of old people. We can steal one of their cars. But we'll probably have to kill them."

"Yeah," Shirley said.

"You know," Cindy said. "In case one of them rats us out."

Cindy led the way as the girls escaped. They talked about how they would put their sadistic plan in motion. They wanted to find someone old and feeble...someone who could not fight back...someone who they could kill for fun.

"I suppose a good analogy would be to compare the girls to the boys from Columbine who would come over a decade later," Orange said. "One needed the other to pull off such a horrid act. They needed that voice over their shoulder to egg them on. They both wanted the same thing and together they could make it happen."

Both Cindy and Shirley would dye their hair red in order to disguise themselves. They then went "victim hunting," touring Cindy's old neighborhood in Auburn Green, a condo for senior citizens. They wanted a car. A nice one. So they began searching the parking lot for a car and would match the number on the parking slot to the condo number.

Then they would knock on the door. Their questions were innocent. They would ask for directions, a glass of water or ask to use the phone. But there was something about their demeanor, a sinister or insincere look in their eye that set off the alarm bells for all of the senior citizens they met. They were allowed inside by Joe Becker and his wife who gave them a glass of water. When they left, however, the elderly couple immediately washed the glass and scrubbed the phone with alcohol, the girls seemed so dirty.

"They were looking for an easy target," Orange said. "Becker was seventy but still probably too much of a hassle for them. They needed easy."

Then they knocked on the door of Anna Brackett.

"We decided we were going to kill her when we saw her," Shirley said. "She was just an old lady. Just a perfect setup. We killed her because we wanted her car and we didn't want to get caught."

Anna was a retired seamstress who worked for Sears. She had great-grandchildren who were the ages of Cindy and Shirley.

She was a helpful and kind person to all her knew her. She didn't hesitate in helping some girls that were the ages of her great-grandchildren.

"Can I help you?" Anna opened the door with a smile.

"Hi," Cindy said. "Can you please help us? We need to call our parents and the phone down the street is not working."

"Sure," Anna said, opening up her door.

Ann was congenial and didn't see any reason not to trust the girls. She let them into her home and the threesome chatted for over an hour. They sat on the couch and she gave them soda. She would show the girls pictures of her family. Pictures of her children, grandchildren.

"It is unusual for a sociopath to want to know about their victim," Orange said. "They really don't want to know their victim because it humanizes them. So perhaps the teen girls were hesitant at first. But it was more of a case of them working up the nerve to do what they set out to do."

The phone rang and Anna went up to answer it.

The call came from her son.

"I'm on my way," her son said.

"Okay," Anna said, hanging up the phone. "I'm sorry, girls. My son is coming to pick me up. We're going to the bingo parlor."

"Now," Cindy said as the girls pounced.

Shirley grabbed the elderly woman by the throat and slammed her to the ground.

"What are you doing?" Anna screamed. "What are you doing?"

Cindy sprinted to the kitchen and rifled through the drawers. She found a butcher knife and gave it to Shirley.

"Do it," Cindy commanded.

Shirley would then stab the helpless old woman without mercy. She would recall stabbing her in the neck and "freaking out" because the old lady kept screaming.

"You're killing me!" Anna shouted.

"Good," Shirley said, slicing the knife down again. She would stop only when she saw the blood coming out of Anna's mouth.

Anna Brackett would suffer over twenty-eight stab wounds although the coroner believed it could have been more as the blade went through the same entry point. There was one stab wound where the blade had gone in four inches deep past Anna's breastplate.

"She died a horrific death," Orange said. "Painful and horrific. I've read some psychiatrists say that Shirley was getting revenge on all of the people that hurt her in the past, that in some way Anna symbolized her mother and she was killing her mother symbolically. I believe that is psychobabble. Shirley was not that bright. She was following the lead of Cindy and they wanted to kill and maim. That was the point. Not to subconsciously work out her anger. She was a defective unit."

Cindy then sifted through all of Anna's drawers and closets looking for money. They found the keys to the old woman's 1970 Dodge and ripped the two telephones from the wall.

They went into the garage and found out that the keys they had stolen would not start the car. Angered, they left the condo on foot and began hitch-hiking.

Ironically, Anna's son Carl would drive pass them on the street, ignoring the girls who had their thumbs out.

He then entered his mother's home and discovered her mutilated body on the floor.

It was a surreal scene for her son. His mother on the floor in a pool of blood. Trapped in his own real life horror movie, Carl would never have guessed that two underage girls would be capable of such a thing.

LIKE A DAY AT THE OFFICE

Cindy and Shirley made it to her home in Auburn. They turned on the television, eagerly awaiting news of the murder they had committed.

Too many people had spotted them around the neighborhood. In all, eleven people informed the investigating officers of the two red-headed girls with the strange demeanor.

Some remembered Cindy from when she lived with her grandparents in the condo development. The deputies, however, didn't believe that two teenage girls could have done what they did to Anna.

Back home, the girls would cheer as their murder was reported on the evening news.

Then they went to sleep.

At 2:30 a.m the deputies would arrive at the house of Cindy Collier.

Deputy George Coelho didn't believe the girls did the crime. But after a few minutes of questioning, Shirley confessed.

Cindy, however , would not only confess to the crime, she would gloat.

"She started to laugh," Deputy Coelho said.

Cindy expressed little remorse. She told the deputies that she felt like killing more people.

Shirley was excited and giddy as they had done something that "they had never done before."

They were placed under arrest and one of the deputies began reading her the Miranda rights. Shirley interrupted him, repeating the rights verbatim as she was already familiar with the process.

Cindy would tell the police that she felt jealousy toward anyone who appeared happy and normal. She felt such envy that she wanted to kill them.

The deputy expressed shock as Cindy detailed her desires of wanting to hurt people. She bragged about stabbing, shooting and throwing people into the Auburn Damn. The officers knew it was all bravado...with the exception of what they did to Ann Brackett.

The two girls would go to trial in July of 1983...a juvenile court.

What the girls wanted was fame and publicity.

They would get it as the brutal murder would be talked about in numerous high-profile magazines and the court case would reach a national audience. A movie called "Fun" was produced, chronicling the girl's first day together.

CRIME AND PUNISHMENT

Shirley's attorney, Thomas Condit, would enter a plea of not guilty by reason of insanity. "I'd like to say that Shirley felt sorry," Condit said. "But I can't. That's part of her problem. She told me that while she was killing the old lady, she was thinking of everybody she hated—her father and his mother. But the psychiatrist believes it was a symbolic killing of her own mother."

Both girls would receive the maximum imprisonment for underage girls. They would remain in jail until the age of twenty-five then be released.

"Shirley really can't understand the difference between right and wrong," Condit said. "How do you appreciate right and wrong when you have a father telling you it's wrong not to stay home and service him when you should be in school?"

THE AFTERMATH

Cindy would spend the next nine years at the California Youth Authority facility in Ventura. She would obtain an associate of arts degree then go on to study law at Pepperdine University. She would go on to have four children and live in Northern California without any further brushes with the law.

Shirley would be sent to the Central California Women's Facility near Chowchilla.

She would threaten other inmates and her jailers during her time in prison. She spent her days reading romance novels as she tries to take her mind off the tormented childhood which led her to be capable of such a crime.

"I think of my dad and it hurts," Shirley said. "I'll just feel pain and I'll have to cry to get it out. I can't really pinpoint where it's from. God knows, I'll get hurt and just cry."

Shirley would complete her high school education and become a born-again Christian. The attempts to improve her life would prove futile, however.

She had tried to contact her parents but they never returned her calls or letters. Finally, in the summer of 1992, Shirley tracked down the number of her parents in the Pacific Northwest. Louis, the man who had molested her, would answer her call.

They had not spoken in four years but he had told her that her mother had left him a few months prior, leaving the three young boys with him. Shirley asked about her favorite brother, L.J., but her father avoided giving her a straight answer.

Shirley wanted desperately to know what happened to her younger brother but could not locate him anywhere. Her father would then stop returning her calls.

On June 30th, 1995, Shirley would be freed from prison after serving twelve years for the murder of Anna Brackett.

Her father would die in 2002.

Unlike Cindy, Shirley's life of petty crimes would continue. She would get involved in prostitution, theft, and burglaries. She has shown remorse for the murder but also stated that "there is no going back."

Both women are now free, getting leniency for the crime because of their age. Their light sentences would draw the ire of Anna's son, Carl, who would rage at the judicial system that gave his mother no justice.

KILLER TEEN : THE TRUE STORY OF KRISTINA FETTERS

JANET NIXON

Kristina Fetters was the youngest woman in the state of Iowa to get sentenced to life in prison without parole after she murdered her great-aunt. But eighteen years later she would be re-sentenced after the Supreme Court ruled that mandatory life sentences for minors was unconstitutional.

Kristina would later be released to a hospice center as she developed breast cancer in prison.

But what happened that fateful night of October 25th, 1994? Kristina was only fourteen years old, five-feet tall and barely one hundred pounds. Yet she committed one of the most brutal assaults in the history of her Iowa town.

This is what transpired in her life before and after she committed a brutal murder of her loving aunt.

EARLY LIFE

She was born Kristina Joy Fetters on February 5th, 1980. The product of a biracial union between her mother Darlene and an African-American man, Kristina did not get to know her father growing up.

Instead, she spent her childhood with Arlene and Wayne Klehm. They were the great-aunt and great-uncle of Kristina but she thought of them as her grandparents. She would refer to Wayne as "Uncle Sheenie" and to her aunt Arlene as "Pooper."

Kristina would play at their home as a young child, swinging from bedsheets tied to a tree in the front yard of the couple's one story home.

Wayne was the easy going one of the couple. Arlene, on the other hand, was the one who enforced discipline on the precocious Kristina.

But Kristina was close to her aunt as were all of her other cousins. Arlene was described as a 'spitfire', a woman who spoke her mind.

"Arlene was just a tiny framed, little woman that would tell you exactly where to go and how you could get there," Kristina's cousin Shanna Sickles said.

Kristina would not meet her biological father until she turned eight years old. She wanted a close relationship with him but the bond never materialized.

"I want him in my life," Kristina said to the Iowa Register in 1996. "I need him in my life. I don't think he knows what he wants."

RUNNING WITH A BAD CROWD

Kristina seemed to have little guidance in her early life. At only twelve-years old, she would meet a twenty-three year old African-American man from Milwaukee named Anthony Leon Hoover. He was a gangster "wannabe", seeking membership into a street gang called the "Black Gangster Disciples." Immature and naïve to the perils of the street, Kristina told the man that she was seventeen years old and ran away with him.

But in June of 1993, Hoover would be arrested on kidnapping charges. He held Kristina at gunpoint, broke her nose and then raped her.

Kristina could not cope with the trauma inflicted by the older man. She would not go to school and would runaway on a weekly basis.

By January of 1994, she was so troubled that she was sent to the Orchard Place, an unlocked facility for minors with behavioral problems. Kristin was placed on Prozac and underwent treatment.

"She was on three different medications that are well known to not play well together now," her friend Jaimi Ross said. "She was showing every warning sign, every red flag that you possibly could on these drugs and they were all ignored."

She also sought solace in Christianity to no avail. A Polk County Juvenile Court officer said that Kristina "lived in a fantasy world most of the time."

Her mother, Denise, would support this assessment as she described her daughter as having hallucinatory episodes.

"She'd say 'look, look, there's Johnny. He's laying on the floor," Denise said. "There's a knife in his head. He's bleeding. Somebody help him, somebody help him. And the teachers would try and re-direct her, you know, you need to get up here and finish your homework."

In September of 1994, her Uncle Wayne would die. Aunt Arlene then sent her grand-niece a handwritten letter, trying to smooth things over.

"Let's be nice to each other and forgive me if I hurt you," Arlene Klehm stated in the letter.

But Kristina would not take the olive branch of her great-aunt.

PLOTTING A MURDER

Ten months later, on October 25th, 1994, Kristina and her roommate Jeanie Fox escaped from the Orchard Place.

Their destination was Kristina's great-aunt's home in Polk County, Iowa.

Arlene Klehm was 76-years old and had little contact with her grand-niece since her placement into the mental health facility.

Living in her fantasy world, Kristina concocted the idea that her aunt Arlene had a lot of money. She planned to escape from the facility, kill her aunt and ride off into the sunset in her truck. What her plans were beyond that, she didn't know.

All she knew was that she needed a partner in crime.

First, she approached a girl named Jessica Wilhite. She explained that her aunt had a lot of money and it would be an easy kill. They could take both her money and her truck after doing the deed.

Jessica remained non-committal.

Kristina then went to Tisha Versendaal and told her of her plan.

"She sits in a chair all day," Kristina said. "I'll stab her then cut her throat. She keeps her money in a safe. We'll take all her money then get away in her truck."

But she found no taker in Tish who was due to leave the facility soon. Instead, she settled on Jeanie Fox, who wanted out of the facility.

Telling Jeanie her plan of escaping and leaving the part of killing her aunt out of the equation, the two packed their bags. They left the facility without incident and that is when Kristina told Jeanie of her other plans.

"Do you want to come with me to kill my aunt?" Kristina asked.

A FIELD TRIP TO MURDER

The girls stopped at three different homes before heading off to kill her aunt. The final stop was at the apartment of a friend where Kristina got a small paring knife.

"What do you need that for?" the friend asked.

"I'm going to kill my aunt," Kristina laughed as she left the apartment.

The two girls arrived at Klehm's home and noticed that a van was parked outside.

Her aunt was entertaining company.

Kristina wanted to wait as she didn't want any witnesses.

The two girls then knelt behind a fence and waited for her aunt's friends to leave.

"I am going to fucking kill her," Kristina repeated the sentence like a mantra outside the home. "Satan has given me the power to do so."

Her aunt's visitors finally left and the two impatient girls knocked on the door. The old woman let them both in, unsuspecting of what the girls had in store for her.

The three small-talked in the kitchen before Kristina pulled Jeanie into a side room.

"I'm going to fucking kill her," Kristina said, again like a mantra as if she were psyching herself up.

Gathering up the nerve, Kristina marched into the kitchen where her aunt was sitting and smashed her over the head with a tea kettle.

Arlene fell to the ground. She tried to get up, woozy, and asked what happened.

Kristina showed no mercy. She exchanged the kettle for a heavy metal skillet and smashed it across her aunt's head.

"Give me the knife," Kristina called out to Jeanie.

Taking the paring knife, Kristina tried to slice Arlene's throat but the knife wasn't sharp enough. She then rummaged through the kitchen drawers, found a larger knife and stabbed her aunt in the back.

"Anthony!" Kristina cried out with every stab (according to Jeanie). "Anthony! Anthony!"

"Help!" Arlene wailed at Jeanie who stood and watched. The bloodied woman wobbled over to the phone but Kristina got there first.

"No!" the teen girl said, ripping the phone off the hook.

Kristina would stab her aunt a total of five times in the back. There were also defensive wounds on her hand and lumps on her head.

Her aunt now dead, Kristina wanted a change of clothes. But first she rummaged through Arlene's bedroom, stealing her necklaces and other small pieces of jewelry.

"We need to find her damn keys," Kristina called out to Jeanie.

They searched for the keys to both the safe and the truck to no avail.

Kristina then thought she heard police sirens in the distance. The two girls began to run and Kristina started to cry.

The girls ran down the block, pounding on the doors of neighbors until police arrived.

"I killed my aunt," Kristina sobbed. "I killed my aunt."

"It was a grisly scene," Detective Neil Schwartz recalled as he came upon Arlene's body. "Brutal. Very bloody."

THE AFTERMATH

Kristina would be charged with first-degree murder and her case was transferred from the juvenile system to a district court in order for her to be tried as an adult.

Her defense team would enter a plea of insanity. She would undergo psychiatric examination with Dr. Michael Taylor who stated that he didn't think Kristina was insane but rather had a personality disorder.

Her planning was too precise and her deception upon entering her aunt's house did not suggest that she was insane, the doctor explained. Furthermore, she understood what she had done after the killing.

But another psychiatrist, Dr. Gaylord Nordine, believed that Kristina was in a psychotic state caused by the Prozac. Dr. Taylor disagreed, stating that Prozac would not have had any adverse consequences on her and that Kristina was also on Thorazine at the time which should have made more her even more docile.

"In talking with her I found absolutely no evidence of any type of psychiatric disorder, " Taylor said. "And in talking with her I found absolutely no indication that she was doing anything on October 25, 1994, other than killing her aunt."

On December 18th, 1995, Kristina would be sentenced to life in prison without parole.

She would serve out her sentence at the Iowa Correctional Institution for Women in Mitchellville, Iowa. She would file appeal after appeal as her attorneys would bring up the fact that this was cruel and unusual punishment for a juvenile.

According to her friends, Kristina didn't forgive herself for what she had done.

"When everybody else was telling her that they forgave her and they're showing her unconditional love," Jaimi Ross said. "She didn't feel she deserved it. It was very hard for her to accept."

Kristina and Jaimi would becoming close friends in jail. They had to...They were two children in an adult prison who were serving life sentences.

When other children came into the facility, Kristina and Jaimi would serve as mentors of sorts.

"They came in and everybody would share their story. It would be Kristina, myself, and another inmate. We'd just open ourselves up and let it all pour out and let them see us for the same flawed humans that they are."

A TERMINAL ILLNESS

In 2013, however, Kristina would be diagnosed with inoperable breast cancer. By November of that year, Kristina would be re-sentenced to life in prison with the possibility of parole.

The judge also recommended that she be immediately paroled due to her illness.

The decision on whether or not to set her free set off a firestorm of controversy in Kristina's own family and the state of Iowa.

"To give her her last few moments of joy and peace," Kristina's mother Denise Fetters said. "I think could be the best thing that she could receive."

But other family members weren't so keen on that idea.

"I just don't feel bad for Krissy for where she's at," Kristina's cousin, Shanna Sickles said. "She put herself there. She didn't give my Aunt Arlene the opportunity to die with her loved ones. Bottom line, if you get life in prison without the possibility of parole, it's life."

But Kristina also had her supporters in friend Jaimi Ross.

"I completely understand when people say things like 'Oh, a life for a life, she took a life, she should die in prison,'" Ross said. "That states more about where you're at in life, and not her, not me and not her family. I get that that's where your heart is and that's what you believe. Were not asking for her to have a second chance."

The parole board decided to release Kristina on a hospice-only basis. There was outcry from people who wanted her to stay in jail, stating that the prison only set her free to save on medical costs.

In the end, the bureaucracy mattered little as Kristina had already reached stage four with her cancer.

"No one can alter the past," Kristina's aunt Darcy Olson said. "It is what it is, this happened to our family and it's now time for my family to have closure. Kristina's impending death cannot be denied and while there have been negative comments, we believe, as the victims, our family has suffered enough and we ask the parole board to grant our request."

Darcy was the only family member aside from Kristina's mother that supported her during the trial and parole hearings.

"It's just so bitter sweet," Olson said. "This has been a 19-year old tragedy for my family. This will bring closure for my whole family and help us all cope just a little bit better with the situation."

"Everybody's like, well, she was a monster," Ross said. "She was evil. It would be so easy in this world if that were just the case. But that's not the way that it is. Not everybody that commits a crime...not everybody that's a sinner is evil or a monster. Her legacy, I hope, will challenge other people to see what they can do for kids. For teenagers. Before it gets to the point where they're in prison or needing to go before a judge for any reason."

The cancer would spread throughout her bones and spine. Kristina would live out her last days in pain.

"The screams I had to listen to last Sunday, no mother should ever have to hear in her life," Kristina's mother, Denise said.

Seven months into her release, Kristina would die at the age of thirty-four.

BRITTANY HOLBERG

Brittany Holberg was a twenty-three years old prostitute when she was convicted of murdering 80-year-old A.B. Towery Jr, stabbing him over sixty times.

The controversy surrounding the case centered around the relationship of Brittany and Towery prior to the killing. Brittany argued that Towery was a client who went into a rage when he found drugs on her person. He attacked her and she retaliated in self-defense.

Further investigation would reveal otherwise, however, as Brittany would use numerous household items in a brutal assault on the elderly man.

She fled the scene only to be caught at a McDonald's after police received a tip from a witness who saw her on "America's Most Wanted."

With her good looks and well-proportioned body, Brittany has remained in the spotlight as she was featured in a Maxim Magazine article as one of the "hottest women on death row".

Brittany still sits on death row today with her case being appealed on the numerous levels in the court system.

EARLY LIFE

Brittany was born on January 1, 1973, in Amarillo, Texas.

Accounts on Brittany's home life vary as she would manipulate according to the needs of her listener. To her probation officer, she informed them that her home life was "good" and that she "had everything that she ever wanted". She would often describe her mother as her best friend.

During other occasions, however, Brittany would paint a different story.

She would describe her parents as being "hippie-drugsters". Brittany would state that she was close to her mother but never knew her father, a heroin addict who was in and out of the Texas prison system. Her mother would later marry a man named John Schwartz with the couple marrying and divorcing four times.

They would drink heavily and openly smoke weed in front of the young Brittany who would be sexually assaulted by a babysitter at the age of five. When she was twelve, one of her aunts was murdered and according to Brittany "everything fell apart" at home. Her parents would leave her unattended as they indulged in pot and booze.

"They just stopped working," Brittany said. "They just let everything go."

She would be gang raped by two men who confronted her in an alley behind her home when she was thirteen.

Brittany would then spend the majority of her time living with her grandmother. By the age of sixteen, however, she would run away with her boyfriend Ward. The two would make it as far as California, get married, and have a young daughter named Mackenzie.

The union would not last long, however. Brittany would divorce Ward and move back to her native Amarillo. Ward would take Mackenzie and move to Tulsa, Oklahoma.

Brittany would state that she suffered a knee injury and would become addicted to pain medication during treatment. She would then graduate to harder drugs like cocaine.

In and out of rehab, Brittany's life spiraled out of control. She could manipulate with the best of them, however, and would escape from the Midland Halfway House with the help of a female counselor.

Brittany would hang out with the drug-using crowd and her own habits were out of control. To support her addiction, Brittany began working as a prostitute.

This would put her in harm's way on many an occasion as she would get gang-raped and beaten severely.

The assault would put her in the hospital but she would resume "tricking" when she was released.

"At that point in her life, Brittany was incorrigible," forensic psychologist Paula Orange said."Numerous people had reached to her and tried to help. She had extended family members trying to help. Friends trying to help. Even church outreach workers. All to no avail. The drugs had taken root and she was dead set on manipulating everyone around her. Family, roommates, church members, doctors, dentists, and pharmacists would all fall victim to her schemes to get drugs."

By 1993, Brittany was a full-blown drug-addicted prostitute with the rap sheet to prove it. In April of that year, she would steal a gun from her step-father. She then passed over $1300 in "hot" checks and applied for several store credit cards using a fake name.

Brittany and one of her aunts would run a scam on dentists, lying to them about their pain levels in order to get prescription medication. When the prescription drugs ran out, she would return to street drugs like cocaine and heroin. Arrests would follow and Brittany would be charged in Hale County with drug possession, paraphernalia, and public intoxication.

Upon her release, Brittany would proceed to steal her mother's car and forge checks in her name. The prostitution continued unabated as well as she stole the wallet from one of her "tricks" who pressed charges.

While in jail for the theft, Brittany would be introduced to Ella Gibbs and Patricia Karnes who ran the ministry in the Randall County Jail. The women tried to get Brittany on the right track and introduce her to Christianity.

"I wanted to reassure Brittany that she is a valuable person, that her life has great potential, and that this is the mortal portion of an eternal life," Karnes said. " Brittany is an eternal being and through the many prayers from my [prayer] group [in Lubbock,] I have been led to come back into this child's life to support her here, to encourage her, to find her courage from the Holy Spirit within her, and to let her know that there is a human being mortal person who will stand beside her and see the good in her and support whatever God plans for the rest of your [sic] life."

A.B. TOWERY

Towery was by all accounts a nice man. His son would bristle at the idea that he was Brittany's "sugar daddy".

"Dad wasn't a dirty old man," his son said. "Dad was just trying to help somebody and look what he got, and now she's getting three meals a day and a warm place to sleep."

The defense would later bring up the fact that he once pulled a knife on his son Russell during a temper tantrum. Towery would have a history with prostitutes (according to court testimony). Connie Baker would be a prostitute from the 1980s to 1997 and stated that Towery was one of her clients. Baker would also claim Tower as a client but she also had a history of drug possession and auto theft. Diana Wheeler would also admit to being one of Towery's prostitutes in the years of 1994 and 1995. She had come to his home and he even went so far as to clean the stains off his Mel Mac dinnerware. But Wheeler also had a long criminal history like Baker, arrested for prostitution, criminal trespass and giving false identification to a police officer.

The controversy at the trial was if Brittany and Towery had an ongoing "sex-for-money" relationship.

This would be vigorously discounted by family members.

His daughter-in-law would come to the home and help with some housekeeping. His sons would also visit daily and never report any "ladies of the evening" coming to visit their father.

The picture just didn't fit.

Brittany stated she was sent to Towery's place by a fellow streetwalker who went by the moniker of "Green Eyes" but that it was later revealed that no such prostitute by that name existed. Brittany had lied like she had so many times before.

The two seemed to have met by chance.

COMING BACK FROM THE GROCERY STORE

November 13th, 1996 was another normal day for the 80-year old A.B Towery. He had just purchased groceries at an Albertson's store and was walking back to his apartment. As he entered the courtyard, he was approached by the 23-year old Brittany Holberg.

She asked to use his telephone and Towery consented. He wanted to help the sweet-voiced Brittany and didn't believe that she posed any kind of physical threat to him.

What he didn't know was that Brittany was coming down from a cocaine high and had not slept in ten days.

"Brittany could be persuasive," Orange said. "She was well-versed in how to charm people, she knew exactly what to say and do in terms of body language. She was like a trained actress. It didn't take much cajoling on her part to convince Towery to let her inside his home. He probably thought 'what's the big deal?'"

Once inside, Brittany would demand money from the elderly man but he refused. Brittany then attacked Towery, trying to strong arm the wallet out of his pocket. The struggle began in the living room. The two then pushed and pulled each other around a partition that separated the kitchen from the living room. They then returned to the living room. At some point, Towery tried to leave the apartment but Brittany pulled him back in. The evidence also indicated that the two paused during this 45-minute fight, catching their breath and nursing their wounds. Brittany would sustain minor stab wounds to her stomach and thigh.

"This was most likely a fight that had a lot of clutching and grabbing," Orange said. "There was less blood in the living room so the conjecture is that is where the fight started. There was blood near the door so that suggests that Towery was bleeding out and trying to escape for help. Remember, he was a slow-moving 80-year old man. Brittany was a young woman but she was fueled by cocaine. He's getting tired a lot faster than she will."

Eventually, Brittany gained the upper hand. She used various objects around the home to beat down Towery. She started with a cast iron frying pan, then a steam iron, a claw hammer, a fruit knife, a butcher knife and then two forks. Towery would fall to the floor, a bloody mess.

Brittany then took a lamp and shoved its base five inches down his throat which choked him to death.

Satisfied that he had finally killed Tower, Brittany removed her bloody clothes. She washed up in his bathroom then went to his closet to find some clothes that fit her.

Walking back to his dead body, Brittany retrieved the wallet out of Towery's pocket. She took out the $1400 dollars he had and dropped the now empty wallet onto his stomach.

Brittany casually walked out of the apartment and hitched a ride with a young couple. The couple dropped her off at a local crack house where Brittany paid them off with two $100 bills (which had blood stains on them). Inside the drug den, Brittany befriended the proprietor and changed clothes again. She then went to a local hotel with hundreds of dollars worth of cocaine and indulged.

TRIAL

Brittany's defense attorney, Catherine Brown Dodson, would argue that Holberg acted in self-defense when she killed Towery. Her primary argument was that Towery was far from an innocent, elderly man. He was, in fact, a drug abuser himself who became physically violent with Brittany when he found a crack pipe on her person. He then hit Brittany two times in the head when she turned her back to him. Brittany retaliated and ultimately put the lamp post in his mouth in an attempt to end the fight.

Brittany then fled as she believed that no one would believe her side of the story because she was both a prostitute and a drug addict.

While in jail, Brittany would try to coerce Katina Dixon, her cellmate to kill Vickie Marie Kirkpatrick who was the prosecution witness.

Towery's history with prostitutes would be brought up in court testimony. They would also mention incidents of violence with his ex-wife and children but jurors didn't believe the old man was in any type of shape to employ the service of a prostitute.

"My father didn't even like the word 'sex'", one of his sons said. "He was old-fashioned."

A psychiatrist would testify, however, that Brittany had battered wife syndrome, post-traumatic stress disorder, and cocaine addiction.

The jury did not take long to deliberate, finding Brittany to be a cunning, manipulative liar who committed one of the most brutal crimes in the history of Amarillo.

They would find her guilty and Brittany would be moved to death row at Gatesville, Texas.

"I can't even explain to you," Brittany said in a magazine interview. "What it's like to have someone say 'You are sentenced to die.' It's words. You feel helpless, numb. It's almost as if your emotions shut you down."

Brittany would spend her first few weeks in prison laying prone on her bed in a zombie-like state. Over time, she grew accepting of her situation. She knew she was going to die but made it a point to learn to take each day one step at a time.

Her inspiration for cleaning up her act came from the memory of her daughter Mackenzie.

"I cannot live," Brittany said. "And I cannot die, knowing that my child has to live with the horror that these people tried to say about me, the story of the crime, their depiction that I was a cold-blooded person."

Brittany states that she dedicates her days to reading, writing to family and working on her law appeals. She also is anti-death penalty advocate.

She would follow other Texas inmates who were now on death row and make appeals on their behalf, specifically that of Betty Lou Beets.

"I realized," Brittany said. "It doesn't matter whether I'm guilty or innocent, this has now become a very political thing... At this point, they're just killing to kill."

She complained that after a recent jail uprising, the treatment of death row inmates has worsened.

"You would not believe the treatment we are given," Brittany said. "Just two weeks ago, we were informed that not only would we be strip-searched for our one hour of recreation a day, but also when taken for a shower. So for the last two weeks, we have been stripped no less than six times a day. This is every day, sometimes at times like 2:30-3 a.m., and we never leave the building or our cells for that matter."

As of this writing, Brittany's stay of execution has been appealed and appealed for the past eighteen years.

Her attorneys would exhaust the appeal process in the state system but it is now in the federal courts.

Her case, however, has been costing taxpayers "conservatively to be at least $400,000" according to county criminal attorney James Farren. In the future, he has decided to forgo seeking the death penalty in capital cases.

Farren continues to favor a death penalty but only under certain circumstances like "a guy walks into a day care center and kills the children or if someone kills a police officer or a firefighter in the line of duty."

Farren predicted that Brittany would remain on death row for another five years at least. "They can go through the U.S District Court in Amarillo, then it can go to the Fifth U.S Circuit Court and the U.S. Supreme Court. Then from there it can go back to the U.S. District."

But the appeals can come to a halt if the district judge refuses to hear it again.

"If the Supreme Court says 'no,'" Farren said. "That's when the district judge can feel safe in stopping this process."

The entire process has been an infuriating one for the Towery family. His son both rages and mourns about what happened to his father.

"She tried to apologize to us during the trial," Russel Towery said. " I got up and walked out. I'm sure other families are going through the same things I'm going through. It's been almost 19 years ... people forget."

"I don't want to die before she does. I want to stand there as she's kicking and screaming going to the death gurney. I want her to think about what my dad went through when she didn't even know his name," he said. "She thinks that because she said she was sorry, that everything's all right. ... she is evil and needs to be destroyed."

HUSBAND KILLER : THE TRUE STORY OF KELLY GISSENDANER

45

JENNIFER KENDALL

Kelly Gissendaner, born Kelly Brookshire, became the sixth and last woman executed in Georgia for her role in the murder of her husband, Douglas Gissendaner, by her lover, Greg Owen. The murder was gruesome, Kelly demonstrated a lack of credibility with lies, and the murder was clearly premeditated- three things that helped a jury convict her of her role in the murder. What hurt her the most, though, was that her former lover turned on her and testified against her. Kelly seemingly changed her life in prison, mentoring and preaching to other women. Her legal team appealed the decision due to a lack of proof, her redemption, and her relationship with her children. The mother of three children cried and sang "Amazing Grace" as she received the lethal injection and one hundred people protested her death outside.

Early Life

In 1968, Kelly Brookshire was born to Maxine and Marry Brookshire in Georgia. She has a brother that was born one year after Kelly. Kelly and her brother were not born into wealth or emotional stability. Her family consisted of simple cotton farmers. Her parents drank, did drugs, and fought. Due to the troubled relationship, they did not stay together. Kelly's father left the family and created a new one with no intention of including Kelly into his new family dynamic. This obviously left Kelly feeling unwanted and abandoned. Kelly's mother did remarry a man named Billy Wade eight days after the divorce with Kelly's father was final, but Billy only added more trauma to Kelly's already broken home. Many people came forward with knowledge of sexual abuse to Kelly by her stepfather and other men. On top of the sexual abuse, Billy Wade was physically and emotionally abusive to Kelly, her brother, and her mother. Luckily, her mother also divorced Billy Wade and moved the family.

Kelly stood at six feet tall, and she was rather homely looking. Many people made fun of her for her looks and being "trailer trash". She would prefer to work rather than socialize, mostly due to her household's financial situation and her mother's strict rules. Her first job was at McDonald's. She mostly kept to herself, but the outcast made one friend in a woman named Mitzi.

First child and marriage

Kelly got pregnant with her first child before she finished high school. She claimed that the child was conceived through date rape, and the father was not actively involved in the child's life. She refused to name the father to even her best friends. She also tried to hide the pregnancy for as long as she could, but the reality became apparent around her sixth month. Before she gave birth, her father reached out to her and suggested that she name the child with his last name. Her first child, Brandon Brookshire, was born in June of 1986. Kelly married her first husband, Jeff Banks, at the young age of nineteen, but the marriage only lasted for six months before it dissolved. Reports indicate that the marriage quickly ended when Kelly's father threatened Jeff with a gun for not passing him bread at the dinner table. After the marriage ended, Kelly and her baby moved into her mother's trailer. This was a rough time for Kelly, but she was saved when she met Douglas Gissendaner.

Marriage to Douglas Gissendaner

On September 2, 1989, Kelly became Mrs. Douglas Gissendaner... for the first time. Kelly was four months pregnant on her wedding day, which could have encouraged the nuptials. The marriage was tumultuous from the beginning. They had financial difficulty after they both lost their jobs and were forced to live with Doug's parents for some time. However, Doug provided a good life for Kelly and her child when he decided to enlist in the United States Army. Despite a steady paycheck, Kelly used the money irresponsibly and needed Doug's family to help her with car payments. Doug's parents already didn't love Kelly, and this added to their distrust. When Doug moved to Germany because of his job in the army, it only added to the tension. The move happened only one month after Kelly had given birth to their first child together and her second child, Kayla. When Kelly and Doug were together, they were noticeably miserable. The relationship did not work at all, and they fought constantly. People also spoke up about Kelly's partying and sleeping around with other men while Doug wasn't around. This caused even more strain on the family, and the couple divorced in 1993. This time, Kelly joined the army with no other way to support herself and her children, but she discovered that she was not made for the army. During this time, Kelly became pregnant with another man and gave birth to her final child Jonathan who everyone called Cody. This father would die of cancer shortly after his birth. After returning from the army, Kelly and Doug reconciled. Despite having a child with another man, they didn't want to separate their family. They remarried in May of 1995 and, despite a separation during this time, bought a house together in Auburn, Georgia in December of 1996. A few months later, Doug was murdered.

Greg Owen

While divorced from Doug, Kelly started working for the International Readers League of Atlanta. At this time, she started socializing with her boss, Belinda Owens. When she met Belinda's brother Greg Owen, they had an instant chemistry. The relationship started strong, but it soon started to worry Belinda. Belinda noticed an alarming amount of fighting, and she didn't appreciate the bossy tone that Kelly used when she spoke to her brother. Kelly and Greg broke up, and Kelly went back to Doug and remarried. Kelly and Greg rekindled their romance during a brief separation between Kelly and Douglas, but Kelly ultimately stayed married to Douglas. Many suspect her devotion to her relationship with Doug involved stability for her and her children rather than love. This was only amplified by the fact that many reports indicated that she continued to maintain a relationship with Owen throughout her marriage to Douglas.

Murder and Investigation

In February 7, 1997, Douglas Gissendaner was murdered by in a secluded part of rural Gwinnett County. Douglas came home from a friend's house shocked to find Gregory Owen in his home. Gregory then exhibited a knife and forced Douglas to drive to a remote area. When they stopped, Owen forced Douglas out of the car and made him walk 300 feet into the woods before beating him in the skull with a nightstick and repeatedly stabbing him in the neck and back. When Kelly arrived, she helped set the car on fire to eliminate any evidence.

The night of the murder, Kelly had gone out for dinner and drinks with friends. Despite dancing and having a good time, she went home right around midnight. Friends with her that night reported that she told them that she went home because she had a feeling that there was something wrong. Kelly frantically searched for Doug when he didn't come home the next day. She made several calls, but she reportedly could not locate him. She even called his parents to ask if they had seen him. That same day a missing person's report was created by the local police department, and they started their search immediately.

Investigators had trouble with Kelly's story from the start. When she spoke with them, she described her marriage as happy and noneventful, but other people provided reports of fighting and numerous problems including Kelly's infidelity. One name that came up over and over again in interviews with friends and family was Greg Owen.

Greg Owen seemed to have a reasonable alibi. A roommate stated that he was home all night and got picked up by a friend for work the following morning at 9:00 a.m. With his roommate's alibi, police put Greg's interrogation on hold and continued their investigation.

Investigators finally got a big clue when they found Doug's car. It was left on a rural road in Gwinnett County. The most interesting thing about finding the car was that it appeared to be burned from the inside. At this time, there was no sign of Doug. While the situation didn't look good for Doug, family and friends knew that police were getting closer to the truth.

The day that the car was found, friends and family gathered to the home of Doug Sr. and Sue Gissendaner to support them during this difficult time. Kelly made an appearance, but she didn't stay long. She decided instead to take her children to the circus. While some people can understand how the environment can be traumatic to the children and maybe Kelly wanted to protect them, people found her decision evasive and questionable. Also, shouldn't the children be allowed to mourn with their grandparents? To increase suspicion even more, Kelly went back to work only four days into the search for her missing husband. Her behavior confused people around her. Sure, she had bills to pay, but four days was very soon to go back to work. Many people thought that she was hiding something. Many more people reported a weird attitude for a woman who had a missing husband.

After an already excruciating twelve days for Doug's friends and family, Doug's body was finally found in a horrific condition a mile from where they had found his car. His body appeared to be a bag of trash at first. He was on his knees, bent over, with his face in the dirt. Twelve days of decomposition, the elements, and animal attacks made him virtually unrecognizable. Medical professionals used dental records to confirm that the body was indeed Doug Gissendaner. He had been stabbed four times in the head, neck, and back.

While there was a long list of potential suspects, investigators kept Kelly close. When they talked to her again to go over her initial statements, the pressure must have gotten to her. She finally admitted that she had spoken to Greg on occasion when he called her. She made it clear to police that she did not pursue any relationship with Greg, and he pursued her. She also admitted that she reconciled with Owen during a separation, and she told investigators that he said that he would kill Doug when he found that she was getting back together with him. At this time, she pointed the finger at Greg and police questioned him heavily. Their relationship was officially over.

With the investigation focused on Greg, Greg's roommate changed his story completely. He was afraid that his leis could get him in trouble, and he told the police a new story. In fact, he confessed to investigators that Greg had been gone the night before until 8 am the next morning. With Greg's alibi gone, investigators knew they were getting even closer to the truth.

Kelly's story was raveling apart as well when investigators pulled up phone records that showed 47 calls between the two. They also saw that Kelly initiated the calls 18 times, which goes against what she told them while interrogated that she only spoke to him because he constantly called her. Furthermore, the correspondence ended immediately after the murder. Why would they stop talking so suddenly for no reason? Her inconsistencies made her look bad to the investigators who were suspicious of her story from the beginning.

After more interrogation, Greg confessed to the murder after he was told that cooperation could prevent him from getting the death penalty. He proceeds to implicate Kelly to save himself. He explains how he and Kelly had an intimate relationship, and she told Greg that she wanted him to kill Doug after they settled into their new house. She even came up with alibis at this time. He goes on to describe the murder in detail. He stated that Kelly picked him up and allowed her into his house. She even gave him the nightstick and the knife that he would use to attack her husband. She advised him to make it look like a home invasion and robbery. Greg waited until Doug got home at around 11 pm, and then he forced him to drive out to the boondocks by knifepoint. They eventually stopped, and Greg forced Doug out of the car and told him to walk. He committed the horrible murder by hitting him in the head with the nightstick and then stabbing him repeatedly, leaving him to bleed. Once completed, Kelly arrived with kerosene to get rid of the evidence. After the murder, Kelly told Greg that they shouldn't speak anymore until things die down. This is the confession that Greg gave police. With this confession, Greg only received a sentence of twenty five years to life instead of the death penalty.

As soon as the police had Greg's confession, they went to also arrest Kelly. They barged into her home on February 25th and completed the arrest. Kelly changed her story once again after her arrest. She confessed that she saw Greg Owen the night of the murder. This time she said that he called her, and she went to pick him up. When he picked her up, he told her about the murder. He then proceeded to threated to murder her and her children as well if she did not help him. Even though the police didn't believe her, Kelly maintained her innocence. Greg was only lying to save himself! She even turned down the plea deal offered to her and decided to go to trial. It was the same plea deal that the prosecution gave Greg- a guilty plea would give her twenty five to life, but she would not get the death penalty. Even her lawyer suggested that she take the plea deal, but Kelly decided to go to trial.

Trial

The first day of Kelly's trial was on November 2, 1998. The jury consisted of two men and ten women. Reporters were prevalent throughout the proceedings.

Prosecutors started by painting a picture of a troubled marriage between Kelly and Doug and her affair with Greg Owen. They then claimed that Gissendaner killed her husband to receive the house he bought for the family and two $10,000 life insurance policies. The reward was surprisingly small but substantial enough to be considered a motive alongside her affair. Prosecution also pointed out inconsistencies in her police reports of the night and the fact that Kelly specifically waited until Doug had bought the house for her and her children. She even had the foresight to plan alibis. This indicated that the murder was premeditated.

The prosecution brought many people into court to testify against Kelly. She faced her late husband's father, who was a witness in her trial. He brought up the troubled marriage between Kelly and his murdered son as well as her questionable relationship with Greg. While many people tried to argue that Doug Sr. already disliked Kelly, his closeness to the situation proved effective.

Another witness was Laura McDuffie. Laura McDuffie was an inmate who was in jail with Kelly. While the defense pointed out that the convict may not be the most trustworthy source and McDuffie only wanted time off of her sentence, her claims were convincing. McDuffie confessed that Kelly offered her $10,000 to take the fall for the murder of Doug Gissendaner. Kelly went so far as to provide a map and a handwritten statement of what McDuffie should say. A handwriting expert confirmed that the statement was in fact written by Kelly.

Kelly's own friend Pam was a witness for the prosecution, too. Pam told the jury that Kelly called her and told her that she had killed Doug. She called back at a later time and said that Greg had forced her to do it by threatening to kill her and her children. Pam claimed that Kelly said, "I did it,", but the defense claimed that pam heard incorrectly. Other friends also stepped up to voice they're uneasiness with her behavior while her husband was missing.

The strongest witness for the prosecution, though, was Greg Owen. His statement matched very closely with his confession, but there were certain differences that poked holes in his statement. He originally said that he drove for some time and then Kelly arrived when Doug was dead. He changed the time that Kelly showed up to the murder scene as he was finishing murdering Doug. Doug originally stated that he and Kelly burned the car together, but he then changed his story to say that Kelly simply threw a bottle of kerosene out of the window for him and he burned the car alone. Even with some holes in his original story, the confession remained very damning for Kelly. The former lovers found themselves implicating each other in their once common scheme.

The defense stated that the prosecution could not prove Kelly's innocence beyond a reasonable doubt. Furthermore, Doug Gissendaner was significantly larger than Greg and was also trained by the military. It seemed unreasonable that Doug would obey Greg's commands even if he did have a knife. Greg showed no sign of injury or struggle. It also didn't seem fair that Greg only got a life sentence when he was the one who committed the murder. Also, Greg's testimony, which was part of a plea bargain, gave him incentive to implicate Kelly for a lower sentence for himself.

In the end, a trial of her peers found Kelly Gissendaner guilty after deliberating for only two hours and sentenced her to the death penalty. In just a couple of words, Kelly's life came to an end. However, she was going to do whatever she could to save herself.

Life in Prison

Kelly was taken to prison where she was the only woman on death row. Being on death row, Kelly did her best to retain a relationship with her three children. She also continued to appeal her case, focus on her spiritual health, and mentor other prisoners.

While on death row, Kelly could not socialize with the general prison population. However, she could preach and act as a spiritual guide by talking to inmates through a vent. Mrs. Gissendaner created a bit of a name for herself in prison, and the women inmates supported her throughout her trial. They even called themselves the Struggle Sisters and rallied for her to be taken off of death row and allowed to live the rest of her life in prison.

Execution Reschedules

Her actual execution was actually the third time that Gissendaner had been scheduled for execution. She was previously scheduled for execution at the end of February, but the date was changed due to complications with winter weather. Next, she was scheduled for execution in the first week of March, but the doctors at the prison were concerned because the drug used to perform the lethal injection appeared cloudy. They sent a specimen to be tested, and, in April, they announced the results that there was nothing wrong. Gissenander's lawyers tried claiming that the changes in her execution date constituted cruel and unusual treatment, but the case was thrown out. If anything, Kelly was given more time, but her lawyers fought to the end.

Death

It was 12:21 a.m. on a Wednesday morning in Jackson, Georgia when officials declared Kelly MN Gissendaner dead from lethal injection. Her execution was scheduled for 7:00 p.m., but her lawyers attempted to repeal the decision to the very end. One hundred people stood outside of the Georgia Diagnostic and Classification Center in protest of her death. Her last meal was nachos, chips with cheese dip, and frozen lemonade.

Gissendaner showed remorse for her part in her ex-husband's death until the very end. Her last words were, "Bless you all. Tell the Gissendaners I am so, so sorry that an amazing man lost his life because of me. If I could take it all back, I would." Her words can be interpreted to indicate a sense of guilt on Gissendaner's part. It can also be interpreted to indicate a peace with her position.

Kelly Gissendaner was the only woman at death row for the entire duration of her time incarcerated, and she was the first woman to be given the death penalty in Georgia since 1945- over 70 years. She was one of only six women executed in the state, and she was the last woman to be executed in Georgia.

Appeals and Support

Kelly's lawyers made a valiant attempt at an appeal. In fact, the appeal was more than fifty pages when they turned it in, and it had statements from a number of different people, including inmates, the pope, and political figures.

After being approached by Mrs. Gissendaner's lawyer, the pope responded in a letter stating, "While not wishing to minimize the gravity of the crime for which Ms. Gissendaner has been convicted, and while sympathizing with the victims, I nonetheless implore you, in consideration of the reasons that have been presented to your Board, to commute the sentence to one that would better express both justice and mercy."

The endorsement by the pope was powerful, but the Catholic Church had also just recently vocalized a stance against the death penalty. Even former Georgia Supreme Court Chief Justice Norman Fletcher stood up for the defendant saying that her role in the murder did not constitute the death penalty. In addition to these endorsements, 90,000 people also signed a petition to support Kelly. Kelly's lawyers showed the courts that Kelly showed remorse and represented a criminal who had turned her life around to bring positivity to those around her. They argued that her presence was significantly greater than her absence to those around her, especially her children and other inmates.

Mrs. Gissendaner's lawyers attempted three appeals to the U.S. Supreme Court, but they were denied all three times. Unfortunately, on the day of the execution, Mrs. Gissendaner's children had to choose between saying good-bye to their mother or appearing in front of a judge for one last attempt to appeal her case. The last time that they saw their mother was two days earlier on Monday. In the most heartbreaking of all testimonies, Kelly's daughter, Kayla pleaded with the court to save her mother's life. She made the point that she had already lost her dad, and he would not want her or her siblings to endure any further loss by also losing their mother. Despite the emotional appear and strong endorsements, the court did not waver on its original decision.

Despite the support from multiple sources, Douglas's family, especially his father, maintained throughout the trial that they trusted the legal system and agreed with the sentence of the death penalty. They reminded the public that she chose to go to trial instead of pleading guilty. They also reminded the public that Douglas did not get any choice in what happened to his life. After the gruesome death of their son, an exhausting and emotional search for the truth, and a prolonged trial, Douglas Gissendaner Sr. and Sue Gissendaner got justice.

Death Penalty Debate

Kelly Gissendaner's case became famous across the nation because of its legal implications regarding the death penalty. People for the death penalty noted that Kelly had orchestrated the entire murder, she helped dispose of the body, she lied multiple times, and the family of Douglas Gissendaner deserved justice. People opposed to the death penalty noted that there was room for doubt, she technically did not commit the murder, the person who did commit the murder escaped the death penalty, she showed remorse over her part in the murder, she experienced trauma in her childhood, and she regularly preached and encouraged other women in the prison. Men and women all over the country debated the case, but, ultimately, the death penalty ruling was honored by the state of Georgia, and Kelly was executed while she sobbed and sang "Amazing Grace". She was 47-years-old.

WENDI ANDRIANO

Chapter 1

A dying husband needs a devoted wife. But when love runs out, marriage becomes a burden.

On October 8, 2000, Wendi Andriano snapped. She had played the part of devoted wife to her terminally ill husband, Joe Andriano, for years, but when the love left their marriage, so did Wendi's patience for her husband's eventual demise.

Wendi had a plan to help nudge nature along, and when her plan b expired, she took matters directly into her own hands and bludgeoned him to death.

Wendi first tried to poison her husband by spiking his last meal, a homemade beef stew, with sodium azide, but Joe Andriano did not ingest enough to kill him, only enough to vomit it back up. Wendi then grabbed the nearest object, a bar stool, and beat her dying husband over the head so many times that parts of his brain became exposed.

After thinking she had successfully killed her husband twice, Wendi then realized that Joe was still breathing, so she took a knife from the family kitchen and stabbed him in the side of the throat.

Minutes later, Joe was finally dead.

This bizarre and frantic way Wendi killed her husband isn't the strangest thing about the case though. Known even to Wendi, Joe was due to die from terminal cancer within the next few years anyways.

Why Wendi couldn't wait to kill her husband is an intriguing tale wrought with sex, lies, and strangely, a lack of patience.

Chapter 2

Wendi and Joe Andriano grew up together in the small farming community of Casa Grande, Arizona. But while they both had gone to the same school, they never dated. As a minister's daughter, Wendi's social life was restricted to her father's church. Her celebration for graduating high school was even in the form of a missionary trip to

Mexico in 1989. When she returned she took a job at the local clerical hospital.

Wendi met Joe in 1992 through friends. Although when the couple started dating Joe's family found the minister's daughter to be an unusual fit for the loud, outgoing former football player, they all thought she was friendly enough and approved of the match.

Joe worked for a local boat builder. He was very mechanically inclined and was a very good welder. He owned his own boat and took Wendi for several cruises around the local hot spots for speedboats. They were inseparable.

The couple married in January of 1994. Their wedding took place in a baptist church across the street from their shared elementary school. Their reception was at the Elk's club and was populated by their many friends and family. Even after two years of dating, though, Joe's family felt like they didn't know his new bride very well, but Joe seemed to be very happy, so they were happy for him.

Soon after marrying, the couple became business partners when they started a small company that did windshield repair and replacement. The business combined Wendi's office experience with Joe's mechanical experience, skills they both exceeded at, and the business thrived.

The couple hadn't been married a whole year yet before they faced their first major challenge together. That fall, Joe noticed an odd bump on his neck. When he had it tested, he was told it was a non-cancerous benign tumor, but it wasn't long before they were second-guessing the diagnoses. A year after it was removed, the tumor grew back.

A second surgery and round of tests seemed to reconfirm that the tumor was benign, but shortly after Wendi gave birth to a son in 1997, the tumor was back yet again.

The third time the tumor returned, Joe's wife and family were convinced that the tumor had to be cancer. This fear was confirmed in 1998 when Joe underwent surgery to have the bump removed for the fourth time. Joe's pre-surgery chest x-ray showed that not only was the tumor cancerous, but that the cancer had now spread across Joe's throat, chest, and lungs.

The prognosis wasn't good—Joe had a rare form of cancer and while radiation and chemotherapy were standard, there was no guarantee they would work. On top of this, Wendi was also pregnant again and was only months away from giving birth to the couple's second child.

Chapter 3

In an effort to increase Joe's chances of survival while decreasing his suffering, Wendi and Joe decided to pursue holistic treatments before resorting to chemotherapy and radiation. They had been told that chemotherapy and radiation treatments would likely not cure Joe, but they would lengthen his life by a few years; however, these years would be anything from pleasant. The horrific side-effects chemotherapy and radiation treatments cause are well known.

So the Andriano's decided first to try anything from special diets to alternative medical treatments to prayer—anything that had a chance to help Joe. Joe even attended a holistic treatment centre for cancer patients in Colorado for a few weeks where he was surrounded by other men and women facing the same prognosis as him. After seeing the bravery of others in the same position as him, Joe began thinking about his future again and began to see it as bright for the first time in a while.

After Joe returned from his holistic healing getaway with a bright new attitude, the Andriano's decided the next best step would be for Joe to begin chemotherapy treatments. He had begun to crave his future and was ready to take steps to achieve it. Unfortunately, taking these steps meant that Joe needed to quit his welding job as well as his own position in the couple's business.

To help make ends meet, Wendi returned to working for the first time since the birth of the couple's children. She ended up taking multiple jobs and worked long hours while continuing to care for her husband at home. Eventually, Wendi landed a job managing the San Riva apartment complex in the Ahwatukee foothills, an upscale neighbourhood outside of Phoenix.

Wendi's new job came with some major perks—the salary was above average, which was nice as Wendi was now the family's breadwinner, and it required Wendi to live on site, which meant that the family now lived in a luxury apartment but paid no rent. Wendi's new job also gave her a new life. A large part of her duties as complex manager was arranging social activities for the other residents of the San Riva apartments, who were mostly young, wealthy, single businesspeople.

Every Saturday the complex hosted picnics, pool parties, or late-night socials. The residents even had their own baseball team. Wendi was required to attend every event, which meant Joe was needed to stay home with their two children. Wendi enjoyed this alone time so much that many of the residents at the San Riva had no clue she had a dying husband and two children at home. She partied like she was single.

The first few months at the San Riva went well. Wendi organized mixers and pool parties for the tenants while Joe took care of the kids. Despite being very weak from treatments, he did everything he could, he wanted to do it. He preferred to have his kids around him even when he didn't feel good.

Although they had never gotten close to their daughter-in-law, Joe's parents also pitched in with babysitting so the couple could have time alone together. They didn't get to see each other much as Wendi began spending more and more time at work. Her new job had also given her a new confidence, and she spent many nights out on the town dancing and drinking away her weekday stress with friends. Joe began to fear that Wendi would soon leave him for her new lifestyle, but this fear got sidetracked when his health continued to fail.

In the summer of 2000, when tests revealed his cancer had spread yet again, Joe and Wendi decided to increase the frequency of Joe's chemotherapy. Joe agreed to undergo more treatments, but they quickly took their toll. He lost 15 pounds in the first week alone, and Joe's doctor became concerned. It went from bad to worse very quickly.

By the beginning of October 2000, it became harder and harder to remain optimistic about Joe's chances of beating his cancer. It became apparent it was terminal, but doctors insisted that with treatment Joe could live for several more years.

No one had any idea that Joe would be dead after only the first week of the month. No one, that is, except for one person—Wendi Andriano.

Chapter 4

Just after 2:00 a.m. on October 8, Wendi Andriano called a friend who also lived in the San Riva apartment complex. She told her friend that she needed someone to stay with the kids while she took Joe to the hospital. When the friend arrived, she found Joe on the floor, barely alive.

Joe was on the floor in the fetal position. There was vomit on the floor around him and he couldn't stand up. Wendi confided in her friend that she told Joe that she had called 9-1-1 and paramedics were on the way, but this wasn't true. After seeing Joe in such poor condition, the neighbour urged Wendi to call paramedics. She then went outside to wait for them to arrive while Wendi waiting with her husband.

Wendi did call 9-1-1, but when the EMT's arrived minutes later, she refused to let them or her friend inside the apartment. She said that her husband was dying from terminal cancer and had a do not resuscitate order. Joe was not to receive any medical attention.

Just over an hour later, at 3:30 a.m., Wendi dialed 9-1-1 a second time. The same team of paramedics came to the house. It didn't take them long to realize something wasn't quite right, so they contacted the police department. Both the paramedics and the police were shocked to find out that Joe, who had been terminally ill from cancer for quite some time had died, but not from the cancer that had been slowly killing his body. He died from being repeatedly beaten with a bar stool and from being stabbed in the neck.

When the police opened the front door of the apartment, they were confronted with obvious signs of a deadly struggle. The apartment was in a complete state of disarray, and there was blood everywhere. Blood had been traced throughout the kitchen, the dining room, and the living room of the luxury apartment, and blood had spattered across the walls the ceilings. Lying in the middle of the bloody scene was Joe, with a knife wound in his neck and holes spattered across his visible skull.

While crime scene technicians surveyed the apartment, phoenix police took Wendi down to the station for a formal statement. She was wearing clothes drenched in Joe's blood and was armed with a story that explained how Joe's death had been a complete accident.

In the interrogation room, Wendi told police she and joe had spent the evening in Casa Grande visiting with Joe's parents. They put the kids to bed after they returned home, which was when Joe noticed something odd about Wendi's appearance—she wasn't wearing her wedding ring.

According to Wendi, Joe worked himself into a rage and began accusing her of having an affair. This argument turned into a shoving match, and when Joe grabbed a belt, Wendi grabbed a bar stool and swung. Joe went down on all fours so she hit him again. It was then that she called her neighbour for help. Joe may have been in a terrible state when the neighbour saw him, but according to Wendi when she went outside Joe had gotten back to his feet easily.

Wendi said she denied the EMTs access to the apartment because she and Joe were both embarrassed about the fight, but just minutes after the EMTs left, the fight got physical again.

Wendi said that her husband tried to strangle her with a telephone cord and she defended herself with the first weapon she could get in her hands—a kitchen knife. She was vague about how the knife ended up in Joe's neck though, saying she was holding the knife up when Joe suddenly fell flat on his face. The next thing she knew, blood was spurting everywhere. He must have fallen on the blade, it was simply an accident.

Many things about this story didn't make sense to the police. First of all, the timeline presented in Wendi's story didn't match the accounts of Wendi's neighbour or the EMTs. Wendi's neighbour had seen no evidence of a physical fight when they first entered the apartment—there were no broken bar stools or blood like later when the police arrived. As well, Wendi had few injuries on her body, definitely no injuries that would necessitate self defence in the form of murder.

Joe's illness also shed doubt on Wendi's story. Joe's parents told police that when the Andriano's visited earlier that evening, Joe had been so weak from his treatments that he could barely stand. They had spent the evening doting on their sick son, bringing him any comforts he wanted. If he was too weak to stand, he certainly couldn't have been strong enough to violently attack Wendi.

Police also uncovered a damning piece of evidence from Wendi herself, in a moment when she thought she was all alone. The investigators that had been questioning Wendi left her on her own in the interrogation room for some time while they fact checked some of her statements and checked in with the investigators who were scanning the crime scene for evidence. During this time, Wendi made a phone call to a coworker at the apartment complex and asked them to hide some of her files from the police. This immediately led to a search of Wendi's office where police found evidence that Wendi had in fact killed her husband. She had even been planning it for months.

Chapter 5

While both investigators strongly believed that Wendi Andriano was responsible for Joe's death, they were stumped by her motive. Why would Wendi kill her dying husband? The police didn't know, but they did have one intriguing lead—the phone call Wendi had made from the interrogation room. They were determined to find out what she was trying to hide.

When they searched her office, police discovered that Wendi had been disciplined at work for using her computer to search inappropriate items on the internet while on the clock.She had been conducting research on poisons, and how to use certain poisons to kill people. They also discovered the papers that she had tried to hide—shipping notices for a substance known as sodium azide.

Sodium azide is a lethal substance with a variety of industrial uses including propelling airbags. It is not, however, something that the average person can simply go out and buy. It's not restricted to the point where only certain companies can possess it, but it needs to be bought for a reason—something that an apartment complex didn't have. But based on the information on the shipping invoice, Wendi had found a way around that.

Wendi had created a fictitious business license using the tax ID form for the apartment complex. Using a Xerox machine and an exacto knife, Wendi had removed all information specific to the apartment complex and inserted fictitious information for a fake company.

The business name on the shipping notice was bogus, but the address wasn't. Wendi had the substance delivered to an address in Scottsdale, Arizona in an attempt to distance herself, but that plan didn't work. When the police tracked down the real address on the invoice, workers at the company positively identified Wendi as the person who had come by a couple weeks earlier to pick up a package she had mistakenly had shipped there instead of her own office.

Wendi's coworkers had seen her with a package but that she had been very mysterious with the contents. She refused to tell anyone what was inside. Had this been the sodium azide? And if so, where was it now?

Chapter 6

Suspecting that Wendi had tried to poison Joe with the sodium azide, police took samples of every medication and food they could find in the Andriano's apartment. If Joe had ingested poison, it would have explained the awful state Wendi's friend had seen him in just over an hour before he died. Luckily, the remainders of Joe's last supper, homemade beef stew, still sat in a pot on the stove.

However, police didn't find any evidence of Wendi's mysterious package, or any evidence of the sodium azide itself in Wendi and Joe's apartment. They had just begun to lose hope in finding the poison when they found out Wendi had a storage space in the building that she failed to tell the police about. Hidden behind a stack of boxes in Wendi's storage unit was a small bottle of white powder and a measuring spoon. The white powder was soon identified as sodium azide.

But the storage unit wasn't the only place investigators found the lethal substance—it was also in Joe's stomach contents and in the beef stew on the stove.

While discovering the poison helped police understand that Wendi had been trying to kill her husband, it didn't explain why she had bludgeoned him to death on October 8, 2000. Wendi had spent a lot of time researching poisons and she spent a lot of time manufacturing documents so that she could purchase the poison. It certainly wasn't a spur of the moment decision.

But why would Wendi beat and stab her husband if she had already poisoned him? Prosecutors had a theory, one that would cut to the heart of the crime. It was patience—or more precisely, Wendi's lack of it—that had killed Joe in the end.

Wendi had grown tired of waiting for the cancer to kill Joe, so she decided to give nature a little nudge by poisoning his supper. But according to the theory, when Wendi gave Joe the poison, things didn't go quite to plan. Joe hadn't ingested enough poison to kill him when he began vomiting it back up. With her plan quickly failing, Wendi panicked. She snapped.

Now improvising, Wendi beat Joe with the nearest object she could get her hands on—a bar stool. Pathologists were able to conclude that Wendi beat Joe over the head with the stool no less than twenty-four times. This beating did render Joe unconscious, but still didn't kill him so Wendi grabbed a kitchen knife and stabbed him in the part of his body that caused all this trouble in the first place—the side of his neck.

Chapter 7

Ten days after she murdered her husband, Wendi Andriano was formally charged with first degree murder. Wendi's crime was viewed as being especially cruel due to the large amount of suffering Joe had had to endure over several hours thanks to Wendi's actions. Because of this, the prosecutor's on Wendi's trial did the almost unthinkable, they sought the death penalty.

When Wendi a walked into the Arizona courtroom on September 9, 2004 she looked vastly different from the perky apartment manager that the residents of the San Riva apartments used to know.

At the time of the killing she had been blonde, she had short hair, and generally appeared to be much younger and cute than the individual who appeared in court with long dark hair and thick glasses. Previously, she had liked to look good and show her figure so her conservative dress at the trial was certainly different from the look her friends were used to seeing. She was trying to look more conservative, more innocent.

She had had plenty of time to perfect her new look—it had taken prosecutors almost four years to bring the case to trial. It had been postponed about 12 times before it was finally brought before a judge and jury.

In their opening statement, prosecutors reminded the jury that at the time of the murder Wendi had been anything but the perfect mother or wife she claimed to have been. She had been someone who had no disregard for her husband at all. While her husband was dying, she had gone out partying and started affairs, and when his condition worsened, and it began to cramp her style, she turned to poison.

Wendi didn't like her new role as family breadwinner, especially with the loss of Joe's income, and with rising medical bills, the family was in the worst financial state they had ever been in. Wendi had thought she was going to be able to be a stay-at-home-mom for the rest of her life, and she did not adjust well to her return to the workforce. So Wendi had found an out.

Although Joe did not have any life insurance, even though Wendi had asked several friends to pretend to be Joe in medical exams so he could be insured, Joe had filed a malpractice suit against his former doctor who had continually told him his tumor was benign when it was in fact spreading throughout his body. If Joe died and the lawsuit went through, Wendi would likely walk away with a multi-million dollar settlement.

More than money though, Wendi had wanted freedom. She wanted the freedom to be single again, she wanted freedom to the ball-and-chain who was slowly dragging her spirit into his grave along with himself. Wendi wanted to not have to care about her dying husband anymore, who was too weak to provide her with any love.

Wendi maintained her plea of innocence throughout the trial, and her defence team attempted to prove she had been the victim of abuse not only on the night of Joe's death but also throughout the couple's entire marriage. To explain the poison, Wendi told the court that Joe had been the one who had grown tired of waiting for the cancer to end his life, and had asked Wendi to help him do it himself.

On the witness stand Wendi said that Joe had willingly taken the poison, but she also stuck by the story that she had originally told police, that Joe had suspected an affair and became enraged when she affirmed them. He became deranged and attacked her, starting the bloody fight. Wendi claimed Joe had died during the ensuing struggle.

Wendi's story wasn't enough to convince the court though, and on November 18, 2004 she was found guilty of the crime. It had taken the jury only two-and-a-half-hours to come to its unanimous decision. Six years after her husband joe had been diagnosed with terminal cancer, Wendi Andriano faced a possible death sentence of her own.

On December 20, 2004, the jurors assigned to Wendi Andriano's case met and decided on Wendi's fate—it would be death for Ms Andriano. Wendi, along with most of the courtroom, was aghast. Even Joe's family was shocked by the decision. Wendi Andriano became the second ever woman to be put on death row in Arizona, a state that reserves the death penalty for the worst of the worst.

Wendi Andriano has since attempted to appeal the court's decision, but as of early 2017, all attempts have been denied and Wendi continues to wait on death row. Wendi and Joe's children now live with Joe's parents, who continue to mourn the loss of their beloved son.

Joe Andriano's death was especially long, and especially cruel, but no happy ending was found when Wendi was sentenced to her own death. Many view the conclusion of this case to be the saddest possible outcome. On October 8, 2000, two lives were lost, and two children were left without parents.

HUSBAND KILLER : THE TRUE STORY OF LARISSA SCHUSTER

70

ERIN EDWARDS

70

Larissa Leann Foreman was born January 1, 1960. She grew up on a farm near Clarence Missouri. By all accounts she had a happy childhood. She won first place at the Randolph pony show, her father, Charles, won first place in the men's division and Deeann, her mom, won second in the bareback for pleasure division. Her parents seemed to be very involved in her life. She excelled academically; she was athletic and went after what she wanted with everything she had. She was described as a 'go getter'.

Larissa graduated High school and went on to the University of Missouri Columbia to become a biochemist. She didn't come from a rich family so she would work as a nursing aide at Boone Hospital Center in Columbia Missouri. It's not known whether she liked her work as an aide, however she did like a nurse named Tim Schuster, and he liked her as well. She was electrifying and intoxicating, Tim was enthralled. They started dating after becoming friends and just hanging out together after work.

Finally, in 1982 Tim popped the question, and Larissa said yes. Between 1982 and the birth of their second child Tyler in 1990 there was a whirlwind of things happening. There was the wedding in '82, the birth of their first child, Kristin, and a move to sunny central California, Fresno to be exact.

In the beginning Tim managed the cardiology Department for St Agnes Medical Center. While Larissa worked for Pan Agricultural Laboratories. Larissa saw the company declining and thought it a good time to start her own company; Central California Research Lab. She was ambitious and worked long hours to make her company a success. Tim continued to work at St Agnes and be both Mom and Dad to their two children.

According to friends Bob and Mary Solis, Tim was the one who made sure doctor appointments were kept, homework was done and dinner was cooked and on the table. Larissa ruled her house and Tim having a non-confrontational personality went along with her, if for no other reason than to keep the peace. By this time she was making more than twice what Tim made. It was her money that made it possible for them to move to Clovis and buy a much larger home than the one they had in Fresno. It looked like they had it all...but did they?

By this time Kristen was a teenager and as with most teens there was attitude. Kristen fought with her mother at almost every turn. She stood up to Larissa in such a way that she felt she had no other option than to send her daughter to her parents in Clarence, Missouri. Tim was upset that his wife didn't even discuss this move with him; she'd decided this IS what will happen. And soon his beloved little girl was gone. But still Tim kept quiet.

The Schuster's entered into a bitter, rancorous separation in 2002, after nearly 20 years of marriage and two children. They tried living in the same house after the separation. However Larissa was not happy with this arrangement. From the very beginning she didn't want Tim to have anything to do with Tyler, no visitation and no kind of a relationship with his son at all. This was not okay with Tim. On more than one occasion she made the statement that she wished Tim would just die.

In late June or early July Larissa took Tyler and went on a trip out of state. Tim took this opportunity to secure a condo and move out of the family's home. Larissa was livid that he would have the nerve to leave while she was away and accused him of taking things from the house that didn't belong to him. What earlier seemed like idle threats became something more, she told a neighbor that she should just get it over with and kill Tim herself.

A Plan started formulating shortly after Tim moved out of the Clovis family home. Larissa asked James Fagone a lab assistant and Larissa's sometimes babysitter, sometimes whipping boy if he would help break in to Tim's house and help her get back somethings he took when he moved out. She felt he wasn't entitled to them and left messages on his answering machine telling him he'd better bring them back...or else.

After returning from a trip Tim came home to a house that had been burglarized and ransacked. One of the things missing...the very set of mixing bowls Larissa had had such a fit over. Who was her accomplice in the break-in...none other than James Fagone? Larissa wasn't shy about what they had done, she told her manicurist Terri Lopez, that after the break-in she would go back to Tim's house and sit in a chair and look around at what they had done. She also told Tami Belshay that "it gave her a feeling that was better than sex."

After the burglary the Schuster's relationship went even further downhill. Tim knew who had broken into his condo. Larissa's bitterness not only let her destroy things in the condo, but she even bragged about keying his truck. She said it made her happy every time she saw the marks on his truck. Tim seemed worried about what his estranged wife was capable of. He moved again, this time to a house in Clovis that had motion sensors and an alarm. He obtained a handgun and a permit to carry a concealed weapon. Larissa had told her manicurist Ms. Lopez that she prayed every night that Tim would just die. At one point Larissa told her that she could kill Tim and get away with it. She also asked one of the employees at CCRL if her boyfriend knew anyone that would kill Tim or at least rough him up. She'd made remarks like this before and all who heard them thought she was just venting because the divorce wasn't going the way she wanted it to. She said she would do anything to keep Tim from getting the business.

According to Bob and Mary Solis, Larissa would belittle and embarrass Tim in front friends and family alike. She seemed to relish the power she had over him.

In late June St Agnes let everyone know that there would be a round of layoffs coming and to be expecting it. Tim and his friend Mary Solis was on the short list to be let go. Larissa laughed when she heard the news. On July 9th Tim, Mary, her husband Bob and another friend Victor Uribe all had dinner together. The group broke up about 10pm that night, before Tim left the Solis' they had made arrangements to meet for breakfast the next morning. Tim never showed for his exit meeting or for breakfast. This worried Bob and Mary, it seems Tim was never late for anything, and if he thought he was going to be late he called. He was also supposed to pick up Tyler that evening.

His friends tried to reach Tim, calling his cell phone. Finally they called Uribe and told him that they couldn't reach Tim and would he go by the house and check on their friend. Uribe arrived at Tim's house and went inside. There didn't seem to be anything out of place, until he went to the bedroom. Tim's watch, wallet and cell phone were lying on the dresser. Uribe was now worried as well. Victor said "He never went anywhere without his cell, he kept it with him at all times, in case the kids needed him."

No one knew what had happened to Tim. The police refused to even take a missing person's report until he'd been missing 24 hours. July 10th when Tim had not been heard from in the allotted time Bob Solis filed the missing person's report. Officer John Willow from the Clovis Police Department responded to the call.

Willow found Tim's handgun under a cushion of a chair. He found Tim's cell phone in the bedroom and called all the numbers in his contacts to see if any of them had seen or heard from Mr. Schuster. When he called Larissa she said she hadn't heard from him either. He also talked to Terri Lopez and she relayed to Willow that the Schuster's were going through a rather nasty divorce. John Willow decided to turn the case over to Detectives Larry Kirkhart and Vincent Weibert.

When they entered Tim's home they noted some damage on the wall behind the chair where the gun was found earlier. They found a briefcase in the same room as the chair. Inside they found a microcassette recorder and tape. In the bedroom they found an answering machine that showed only one number, a cell phone number belonging to Larissa Schuster. Detective Kirkhart then asked Larissa to come to the police station for a chat about her missing husband.

During her interview with the detectives she told them that she and Tim were getting a divorce and that they did not communicate very well with each other. They asked her about her cell number being on the caller ID. She fabricated a story about being asleep on her couch and waking up to find she had pushed some buttons and maybe she had speed dialed Tim. They asked her if she had her phone with her and she said no. Kirkhart called for a pause in the interview and went to the parking lot to find Larissa's car. He looked in the window and saw a phone on the center console, dialed her number and the phone in the car rang.

Kirkhart went back to the interview room and asked Larissa to come with them to unlock her car and retrieve her phone. Back inside the station the interview resumed. The detective went through her contacts that she had on speed dial, none of them were Tim's number.

Larissa's whole demeanor changed, she was shaking and in the opinion of the detectives showing signs of deceit. She came clean and admitted that she had lied to the detectives and she knew she shouldn't have. She claimed she wasn't trying to be deceitful. None the less they let Schuster go home, for now. At this point in their investigation they still had no idea what had happened to Tim. Kirkhart had asked Larissa if she thought that Tim could just cash out some money and leave town, go camping or to Vegas to just get away. She told them she didn't think he would do that, that he wouldn't leave his son like that. This was still just a missing person case and most of Tim's friends thought that perhaps he had just had enough, the divorce, the custody battle, losing his job was to much for him to handle. Tami Belshay, Bob and Mary Solis and Victor Uribe were among those friends. The detectives were thinking the same thing at this point.

With no solid leads on Tim's whereabouts detectives Weibert and Kirkhart kept searching for some clue, however small that might give them some direction on finding Tim. Kirkhart was going through Tim's ledger provided to them by Larissa. And they came across a name they were familiar with…James Fagone. They knew his name because he was the one suspected of breaking into Tim's house with Larissa shortly after Tim moved out of the family home a year earlier. They also knew that he was an associate of sorts of Larissa's.

The following Monday Detectives Kirkhart and Daly called Fagone to come and talk with them. Vince Weibert thought that perhaps Fagone might have some "inside" information on Tim's disappearance.

It seems that Fagone was a babysitter for the Schuster's son Tyler, before and after their separation. James was a good kid according to his attorney Peter Jones. "He's an above average student, higher than a 4.0 grade point average…a gentle spirit."

Fagone was nervous during the police interview. He admitted that Larissa had him help her break into Tim's house and take back things that she didn't want him to have.

James told the detectives that Larissa was going around the house looking for things and he just wanted to get the TV and some other stuff so he wasn't paying attention to what she was doing. Obviously James was scared out of his mind by now, but they pressed him more telling him they "knew he was involved somehow" with Tim's disappearance. Fagone's determination not to tell what had happened, what him and Larissa Schuster had done crumbled.

Fagone confessed that he had been there the night that Tim went missing, that he had gone to his house with a weapon. James relayed to them that Larissa had paid him the $2000 to purchase a stun gun and that he could just keep the rest for himself.

So as the day wore on James conveyed the sordid details of the night in questions.

On the night that Tim lost his job at St Agnes and had dinner with a group of friends, James had done what he was told to do by

Larissa, buy a stun gun. Later he would get the call from her (Larissa). She picked him up and went to Tim's house. James laid in wait in the darkness just outside of his door. He could hear Larissa on the phone telling Tim that Tyler wasn't feeling well and she needed him to come to the front door.

A few moments later Tim opened the front door and James sprung from the shadows and attacked him wrestling him to the ground. Tim was struggling; James was using the stun gun on him, on the arm at first, not sure where else he might have zapped him. Soon Tim stopped struggling and when James looked up he saw Larissa with a rag that had been soaked in chloroform.

Were the detectives hearing this right? Was Fagone confessing to the murder of Timothy Schuster? But if they were going to believe any of it they needed some kind of evidence. They asked about the stun gun again, and what had Fagone done with it. He told them he threw it in a portable toilet on the edge of town. The investigators found the stun gun, right where James told them it should be.

Now at the same time Fagone was being interviewed Clovis Police Department got a call from a woman saying that her boss ask her to do something that in retrospect seemed a little off, suspicious even. Her Boss...Larissa Schuster. Leslie Dodd had been instructed to rent a moving truck by her boss. She was told to use her personal credit card and rent it in her own name not her boss's. A year earlier Larissa had asked the same employee to rent a storage unit near Schuster's lab, again to do it in the employees name and with her personal credit card.

Jim Koch got the call to check it out. He went to the storage unit and walked down the hall. He had been told to look for a blue barrel. When he found Schuster's unit and opened the door "there was a very very strong odor." Koch said. "I had on a breathing apparatus and gloves."

He saw the blue barrel, he opened it.

Koch said in an interview, "And when I opened the barrel I—I saw something that was very, very shocking to me and I recognized immediately as human remains. There was a barrel that's over 3/4 of the way full of fluid and portions of—of—body protruding from the fluid. And the body was obviously decaying. It was placed in acid. And the acid was basically eating away at the body."

Had Larissa Schuster killed her husband and put him in the barrel? According to James Fagone, yes she had, and he had helped her and then watched as she poured a caustic solution in on top of Tim. Worst of all, Tim was probably still alive when the acid was poured on him and he was sealed inside the barrel.

Tim had been found, the truth had come out and the Clovis detectives were on their way to Missouri to arrest Larissa for the murder of her husband Tim. They met her at the airport where she had gone to see her family. According to the detectives that arrested her for the murder she didn't even ask what had happened to Tim or how he died.

Both James Fagone and Larissa Schuster were arrested and charged with 1st degree murder.

Now that the perpetrators of Tim Schuster's murder had been arrested it was time to take them to trial. The murder was committed in the early morning hours of July 10, 2003. There was a lot left to do before the trial could begin.

The Clovis police department had to finish gathering evidence, talk to friends and family to make sure that everything was done correctly. They wanted to make sure that Larissa and James would not be let go on a technicality.

The judge had to decide if he would make this a death penalty case or a life in prison without parole case. That would be decided later. The prosecutor had to prepare a rock solid case and present the evidence to a jury in a manner that would guarantee a conviction. The defense would also be talking to people on behalf of their clients. Find people that had nothing but good things to say about them in hopes of offsetting the horrible truths that would come out at trial.

The judge separated the cases and James and Larissa would be tried separately. James was tried first. His attorney portrayed James as a misguided man who hero worshipped Larissa.

He was found guilty and is now serving a life without parole sentence.

There was so much media coverage on Larissa that the defense asked and received a change of venue. Her trial was moved to Los Angeles.

Monday October 22, 2007 Larissa's trial started. Prosecutor Dennis Peterson relayed to the jury of 9 women and 3 men just how the murder went down. He told them that Tim was still alive when the acid was poured over him while he laid head first inside the blue barrel. Her motive? She didn't want to share anything that they built during their 19 ½ years of marriage. She felt Tim didn't deserve any part of the business, or home and didn't want him to have contact with their tween son, Tyler.

CCRL employees would also testify to the facts of the blue barrel being at the lab and the day Tim was reported missing went to look for it and it was gone. They also said that Larissa had said that she should just shove Tim in the barrel and get rid of him.

A large amount of Hydrochloric acid, 12 gallons and Sulfuric acid, 4 gallons was ordered for Schuster's lab, more than ever before. Leslie Dodd (nee Fichera) testified that, "that was more acid than the lab would use in a year."

Joseph Boatwright thought Larissa was joking when she asked "if he thought a body would fit in the blue barrel."

Juror's watched several hours of Larissa's police interview. She made Tim out to be controlling and having a volatile temper. After seeing that part of the interview Bob Solis testified to the contrary, that Tim was very calm and a non-violent, non-confrontational person.

In another part of the interview with Clovis Detectives Schuster stated that "she prayed that Tim would get over this hostility about the divorce." Her manicurist Terri Lopez told a different story. Lopez said that "she told me she prayed every night he would die."

A hair stylist Becky Holland sometimes did Larissa's hair. During those appointments Larissa would rant about Tim. Holland didn't think much about it because she knew they were going through a divorce. Later though she said the hateful remarks escalated, Holland told the court, "this is getting a little creepy. It was so intense."

The jurors got to hear just how intense it was when they got to hear message after message of Larissa calling her husband awful names and making threats about their children. The prosecutor used these recordings to make a point to the jury; Larissa was in a "murderous rage". Nuttall interjected that these messages were left on Tim's machine 7 months before the murder.

And with this the prosecution rested, hoping that they had proved their case. There was one witness that they really needed to be able to lockdown the case against Schuster, they needed James Fagone. The judge had barred his confession so the jury would never hear in his own words what happened July 10, 2003. But he refused to cooperate with Peterson because he had already filed his appeal. The only thing that might have helped Peterson is the fact that James Fagone had already been convicted of Tim's murder.

Nuttall began the defense's case by telling the jury that neither he nor his client could tell them what had happened to Tim because "we don't know". And since the jury heard nearly nothing about Fagone, Roger Nuttall blamed the murder on him. After all Fagone had already been found guilty of the murder Larissa was now on trial for. Nuttall said in his opening statements that "Tim was an angry man who belittled Larissa in over-compensation for his own failings as a husband and father." And that "he began stalking Larissa after the divorce proceedings started."

Now Defense attorney Nuttall brought in a stream of witnesses that would steer the blame away from his client.

He had a medical expert that said the victim's body was cut in half and that the police had completely missed a second crime scene and the evidence from there would have proved that Fagone and others were responsible for Tim's murder not Larissa.

Nuttall even had psychiatrist Stephen Estner on the stand. Estner said that, "My impression was that Mrs. Schuster was a very direct and assertive person, and Mr. Schuster was a more passive and nurturing personality. And I think they started butting heads over that."

Larissa Schuster took the stand in her own defense and adamantly denied the charges saying, "No, I did not kill my husband." Again James Fagone would have the whole murder put squarely on him. Schuster told the jury, ""I heard him say something like 'there had been an accident and Tim is dead.' I thought he was joking."

She said that the $2000 payment to Fagone was for babysitting Tyler and housesitting while she was away on vacation with her son. Schuster said the large amount of acid was for cleaning a large scale of lab glass. Schuster seemed to explain everything away poking holes in the prosecutor's case. Would it be enough to get an acquittal? Had she actually swayed the jury?

It seemed that the trial was plagued with problems, including accusations of juror misconduct. At least one juror was replaced by an alternate due to disruptive behavior. Another admonished for giving Larissa a 'thumbs up' after her testimony. And yet with all of that...it was time for the jury to deliberate of the weeks of testimony they'd heard.

It took a little more than two days for the jury to decide on a verdict.

Guilty of Murder with a special circumstance of financial gain. The verdict came exactly one year after Fagone's.

Roger Nuttall slowed the sentencing of Larissa Schuster while he tried to find reasons to ask for a new trial. He even used the argument that there may have been juror misconduct. Nuttall wanted to talk to the jurors but Ellison said no. Nuttall appealed and the District court of Appeals told Ellison to contact the jurors on Schuster's behalf. All the jurors and alternates refused to speak to her attorney.

So on May 8, 2008, five months after being found guilty of her estranged husband's murder Larissa Leeann Schuster was sentenced to life in prison without the possibility of parole. Judge Ellison also denied her request for a new trial.

At the sentencing a total of seven people stood up to make statements about how they had been affected by the murder of Timothy Allen Schuster.

Kristen, Tim and Larissa's oldest child and only daughter made an emotionally charged statement to and about her mother.

She called her mother a demon for "taking my father away." And told her. "I pray you're continually haunted at night by the sight and sound of my father fighting for his last breathing moments on this earth. I hope you toss and turn and have horrible nightmares visualizing the horrific act of violence you have committed. Maybe later in life I can learn to forgive you, but I doubt it. This is goodbye, not just for now, but forever. This is goodbye as your daughter."

Kristen was so devastated over her father's murder she reached out to a support group murdervictims.com. Several people shared their own experiences of losing a parent at a young age hoping she could find at least a little peace.

ALICIA SHAYNE LOVERA

The life of Alicia Shayne Lovera looked like something out of a soap opera.

Born into poverty, she was ushered into a life of wealth and privilege when her mother married a rich president of a bank. She grew up to be beautiful, popular and spoiled. But she soon find herself in financial ruin when her stepfather committed suicide, leaving the family with nothing.

Her sense of entitlement still intact, she married a struggling math teacher who couldn't resist her charms.

But when the marriage became an inconvenience, she did what all black widows do.

She killed her husband.

This is her story.

EARLY LIFE

Alicia Shayne Good was born in 1966 to teenage parents. Going by her middle name Shayne, her early life wasn't easy as her parents lacked the necessary resources to provide. Her mother would divorce her father. But when Shayne turned seven-years old things to a turn for the better.

"Her mother and she were poor," journalist Jamie Satterfield said. "Her mother met Brent Mills who was a bank president and they married into that family and Brent adopted Shayne."

The change in life circumstance was jarring to the young Shayne. She was instantly given an upgrade in lifestyle as she the world was now her oyster. There were expensive vacations, cars and garish parties.

Her new stepfather, Brent Mills, was a bank executive who treated Alicia and her mother Sandy to all the spoils his job could bring. He was well regarded in the business community and had several contacts.

But Brent had inherited the bank built by his father and lacked his business acumen. He was lenient in granting loans and the bank soon grew insolvent. He was also suspected of using the bank as a money laundering service for drug dealers.

On the surface, Brent told the family that the allegations were all fraudulent. He gave them every assurance that everything would be okay.

Then he killed himself.

"He took a gun to his head and blew his brains out," forensic psychologist Paula Orange said. "That left an indelible image on Shayne's outlook on life."

His suicide would leave the family in financial ruin. The papers would ridicule Mills, giving voice to all of the wild allegations of his mismanagement. The family would be left shamed and with nothing.

The effect was devastating on Shayne. She would go from being the richest girl in the school to being dirt poor.

Again.

Shayne just wanted to get away. She had entertained aspirations of being broadcast anchor, thinking that her beauty and speaking skills would lead to an easy gig. So she decided to move out of state for college. She would attend a university in Missouri where she would meet Kelly Lovera.

They would marry a year later.

The couple would have two children over the next five years despite being the polar opposites temperamentally.

Kelly was cool, calm and wanted a quiet life. He didn't embrace the partying lifestyle that Shayne wanted.

"Theirs was a union that is hard to comprehend," Orange said. "Kelly was not en route to becoming the next bank president. He was a twenty-year old student who was struggling. He wanted to be a math teacher. Shayne wanted to live a hedonistic lifestyle. She wanted to party and spend lavishly. Why they would get married defies explanation."

Bored in Missouri, Shayne would then convince Kelly to move back to her hometown in Tennessee. Kelly would consent to the move.

A RETURN TO POVERTY

The couple would live in Sevierville which was thirteen miles north of her former luxury home in Gatlinburg. But it was light years away in terms of affluence as they were forced to rent out a small, one story townhouse.

The neighborhood they lived in was called "Frog Alley".

"A luxury once experienced becomes a necessity," Orange said. "Shayne had gotten used to living the high life. But married life, particularly one with of a lack of resources, would prove to be difficult for her."

"Frog Alley was a place for the working poor," Satterfield said. "To come back and live there would be extremely embarrassing for her."

Kelly's focus was not on making money. He was working on his master's degree in mathematics while he took a teaching position at Pellissippi College in Knoxville. Shayne would work various odd jobs to help the family make ends meet and was not happy about that.

"She had wild ambitions to become a news anchor," Orange said. "But she didn't do anything to make that happen. She wanted someone else to do all the work for her just like she experienced when her step-father financed her life."

BOREDOM SETS IN

Shayne entertained neighbors for barbecues and poker nights. The problem is, the only people that seemed to come around were other men.

She was thoroughly bored with her marriage and began to have multiple affairs.

"She would flirt with men in full view of the children," Orange said. "Men would come over ostensibly to play cards. She would play 'footsie' with them underneath the poker table. She didn't want to be a mother and got bored with that act. She wanted to party, to be the rich wild girl that she was as a teenager. The idea of staying home with a boring math teacher and two needy children was anathema to her. She wanted a way out."

The affairs would occur in her apartment when Kelly was away. Different men would come and go at various hours.

"He's (Kelly) cramping my style," Shayne told one of her lovers. "And you're so much better than him."

"Thanks," her lover said with a grin.

"Do you know anything about how to poison someone?"

"Excuse me?"

"You know," Shayne said. "How certain poisons are undetectable."

Shayne would test the waters with her lovers. She would ask them about poisons in a joking manner. But then they would soon realize that she was serious. There was an ulterior motive to her affairs.

She wanted to find someone to kill her husband.

And she would find a willing assassin in Brett Rae.

THE NEXT DOOR NEIGHBOR

Brett was young and inexperienced with women. He had never encountered anyone like the sexy Shayne Lovera.

"Brett fell very hard for Shayne," Satterfield said. "Their affair started very quickly. And it was hot and heavy."

"Brett was a rich kid," Satterfield said. "His father was a newspaper publisher (Rick Rae, a Canadian publisher of the Sevier County newspaper). He was a well-to-do guy. He was just wild. He was just one of those people who was 'full-on' all of the time. He was up for anything."

And he was completely infatuated with Shayne.

Shayne set up Brett the same way she set up her other lovers. After a torrid session of lovemaking, she popped the question.

Will you kill my husband?

"I'll do anything for you," he told her with baited breath.

Shayne offered him a deal.

"If he were to get rid of Kelly," Satterfield said. "Then he would get her. That's what Brett wanted."

"Brett let his little head do the thinking for his big head," Orange said. "He was going to inherit money from his father so he had absolutely nothing to gain by killing Shayne's husband. Nothing except sex which of course if he had money, he would have more options than a narcissistic married woman. He simply did not have the life experience to see Shayne for what she was."

She would have a party on November 5th, 1994, an outdoor barbecue with gambling and drinking. Kelly left the party early and went to sleep on the couch.

Brett would be the last one to leave that evening. On his way out the door, they both noticed Kelly asleep on the couch.

"It was a spontaneous thing," Orange said. "They didn't have a murder weapon so they used whatever was immediately available. That would be the baseball bat of Kelly's son."

Kelly would then be bludgeoned to death.

"The plan was to put him in his own vehicle," Satterfield said. "And make it look like an accident."

Brett then dragged Kelly into his jeep and drove down Highway 14. He parked near an embankment and pushed the jeep down the side, watching it carom into a tree.

He then called one of his friends to pick him up.

Brett did not keep the news of the murder to himself. He would brag to two of his friends of what he had done.

"I put him (Kelly) over a hundred foot embankment," Brett said. "I fucked his wife and killed his ass. She told me I'd get more sex and more money if I get rid of him so I did."

Brett told his friends of the other methods he thought of using to kill Kelly but that he decided to beat him to death with the baseball bat then "stage a car crash."

FINDING THE BODY

A pair of tourists would discover Kelly's black jeep below the road. Inside, they would see his bloodied dead body. Initially, they believed that he was the victim of an accident. They called the authorities and reported that it appeared as if his jeep had gone off the road and hit a tree

Park Ranger Jerry Grubb was notified of the "accident" at the Great Smoky Mountains National Park.

The whole scene, however, looked suspicious from the get-go.

"Just wasn't any skid marks," Grubb said. "No disturbed gravel. There just wasn't any disturbance in that area."

Grubb looked inside the jeep and found the body of Kelly Lovera, laying in a pool of blood trailing toward the front seat. The blood should have been trailing behind the victim if he had, in fact, struck the tree head on.

Additionally, Kelly's injuries were not consistent with a car crash victim. The facial injuries appeared to be the result of a beating, not the impact of the jeep against the tree.

MURDER ON THEIR HANDS

The autopsy would reveal that Kelly had been beaten to death and a homicide investigation ensued. Authorities would then visit Shayne's apartment and inform her of her husband's death.

She would go into hysterics, sobbing uncontrollably.

"Do you know why anyone would want to do this to him?" an investigator asked.

"He doesn't have any enemies!" she bawled.

But an officer would notice blood splatter on the glass of Kelly's diploma that was placed on a wall near the couch. They would obtain a search warrant and a crime team would arrive, spraying luminol over the apartment.

Luminol lightens up blood stains when a fluorescent ray is scanned over it.

"The whole living room lit up like a Christmas tree," Orange said. "That is when they knew they had the guilty party."

Detectives then began to question neighbors who all pointed their fingers at Brett Rae, the lover of Shayne.

Both Shayne and Brett were arrested and charged with first-degree premeditated murder.

Brett would confess quickly. He admitted to using the baseball bat and then staging the car wreck. He would be represented by Robert Ritchie who would prep him for the murder trial for nearly three months. Ritchie, however, would notice that Brett was completely obsessed with Shayne. He then turned the case over to Robert Ogle but two weeks before the trial Alan Feltes was brought in as Brett was given joint representation.

"His attorneys were flabbergasted at his refusal to give up Shayne," Orange said. "He was truly in love with her and wanted to protect her even if it meant incriminating himself."

"I did it," Brett insisted. "Just leave her out of it."

Feltes told Brett that there was no way he could win the case with all of the evidence stacked against him. The only thing Brett cared about was putting Shayne in jeopardy.

THE TRIAL

Park Ranger Jerry Grubb would testify against the killing duo, presenting the forensic evidence found at the home and jeep. Friends and family would testify that both Shayne and Brett had bragged to them about what they had done.

Going in desperation mode, Shayne would then take the stand. She wanted to tell her version of what happened that night.

"Brett had stopped by to talk to me when Kelly came out and confronted him," Shayne said. "They began fighting and Brett picked up a baseball bat. He swung it only to keep Kelly away. But then he accidentally hit him and killed him."

Shayne would go on to say that she didn't witness any of this. She was asleep and really knew nothing that happened.

"Brett and I were not lovers," Shayne said. "We were nothing more than neighbors. It was a case of fatal attraction. He had a thing for me and wanted to kill my husband."

She didn't know, however, that when both she and Brett were released on bail they were followed by a Siever County Sheriff. He followed them into the mountains and saw them having intercourse in the woods.

When Shayne was confronted with this evidence, she tried to regroup.

"I had sex with Brett," Shayne said. "But only because I had to. He threatened to involve me in the murder plot. My purpose in going there was trying to save what little bit of life I had left at that point."

The explanation did not go over well with the jury. It took them only an hour and a half to return with a guilty verdict.

OFF TO JAIL

On January 29th, 1996, both Shayne and Brett would be convicted of Kelly's murder. They would not be given the death penalty, however. The prosecution wanted a sentence of life without parole.

Feltes approached by the attorneys for Shayne. They stated that a plea agreement would be possible but it would have to be a package deal with Brett.

Feltes advised Brett to take the deal as the plea agreement would guarantee him a life sentence with possibility of parole. If he didn't take the deal, the odds would be that he would be facing life without parole.

"Just don't do anything to hurt Shayne," Brett said. "I want to see her."

"What?"

"I want to see her before I take the deal."

Brett would persist in wanting to see Shayne. Instead he would take the deal.

"His attorneys described him as having the saddest eyes they had ever seen in a courtroom," Orange said. "He was truly in love with Shayne. She, on the other hand, threw him under the bus. She was willing to say whatever it took to get herself off and it backfired."

THE AFTERMATH

Kelly's children would be placed into the care of his parents. Brett and Shayne would receive life with parole after twenty-five years.

Brett would later try to appeal his sentencing despite agreeing to a plea bargain which barred him from doing so.

His claim would be rejected.

Ray would write that "his trial was ineffective for encouraging him to accept the state's offer of life with possibility of parole; failing to prepare for mitigating circumstances at the sentencing phase; failing to properly conduct a pre-trial investigation; failing to adequately consult with him during critical stages of the proceedings; failing to advise him of his rights to direct appeal and collateral attack of his conviction; deficient performance of counsel at trial; his guilty plea was coerced and involuntary; and his conviction is void as violating the protection against double jeopardy."

"He had conceded his guilt during the guilty plea hearing and that his attorneys did the best they could...he made these admissions only because the attorneys instructed him to do so and although he agreed that he believed himself to be guilty of first degree murder at the time of his plea, he now retracts that admission."

Brett's attorney Feltes would dispute his allegations, stating that he "never had any problem with Brett being incoherent or not understanding anything he was told or advised."

Both Brett and Shayne remain in prison, waiting to be paroled in 2025.

HUSBAND KILLER : THE TRUE STORY OF MARY WINKLER

92

JAMES FALCON

The Case of Mary Winkler

Mary Winkler, at first appearances, would seem to be an altogether normal woman. So too did her family, with a husband who was a Church minister and three young children, girls aged just eight, six and one.

The family lived in Selmer, Tenn., a small town occupied by around 4,500 people, according to the 2015 census. The town is situated to the south west of the state. Not much has happened in Selmer; the most famous person to have been born there was Chad Harville, former pitcher for the Oakland A's, and for one year, the Red Sox. He achieved a 4-9 win-loss record over his career in the MLB.

Today, the most famous- or infamous- person to have come from Selmer is Mary Winkler. In 2006, Mary sparked a border-crossing manhunt, and a court case followed nationwide. She had killed her husband with a shot to the back from the family's shotgun. But it was the gripping, and at times bizarre, court case which gripped the attention of the nation.

Matthew dead, Mary and the family Missing

The date was March 6th, 2007. It was a Tuesday like any other. Mary and Matthew were at home all day together, although Matthew was due to give a sermon that evening.

It was actually members of Matthew's congregation who found his body that night. They had visited his home to check up on him after he had missed the service he was set to give; instead, they found him lying dead, having been shot in the back.

There was no sign of Mary or any of their children at the home, and as such, they were reported missing. The authorities quickly sent out an Amber Alert, since nobody had any idea what could have happened to them, or where they might be. Family and friends had no information to provide police on their whereabouts.

There was every chance that the family had been kidnapped or murdered, and their bodies disposed of elsewhere, although police could not identify a break in, and had no reason to believe that anything of value had been stolen.

It was only a day later that she was arrested in Alabama, having run from the family home with her young children. They were found 350 miles away from home, at Orange Beach, and in the back seat of the van was the family's shotgun. It was certainly suspicious; but what reason could Mary have possibly had for committing such a crime?

The Trial

In the build up to the case going to trial, public interest ramped up. Speculation had been rife about why Mary would have murdered her husband, a seemingly nice, well respected member of the local community. Perhaps either one of them had had an affair, and Matthew had been killed in a crime of passion. Or maybe he had been killed for an insurance claim?

As such, the press reported every step of the story as it came out during the hearing. The trial began when a Tennessee Bureau of Investigation Agent John Mehr read a statement that Mary had made very soon after her arrest. In it, Mary claimed that the couple had been arguing about their family finances, before Mary had shot her husband with their 12 gauge shotgun. She had said that the last thing she had wanted was to actually murder her husband, but she had been brandishing the gun in an effort to convince him to work through their problems, together. The argument had been ongoing throughout the day, and Mary had finally snapped, resorting to drastic measures to be able to convince him. She had never intended to kill him: she had said in the statement, 'I don't want this at all. I don't want any of this to be, at all.'

The statement continued on, and Mary claimed that they had argued often and argued fiercely. 'He had really been on me lately,' Mary had said, 'criticizing me for things- the way I walk, I eat, everything. It was just building up to a point. I was tired of it. I guess I got to a point and snapped.'

At first glance, it would seem that Mary had simply lost her composure, become angry, and killed her husband 'as the red mist had descended'. But after their initial statement, Mary's attorney indicated that there was much more that would come out about Matthew's behaviour when she testified which would help to explain her actions. Clearly, there were more problems with their marriage than the occasional, albeit fierce, argument.

Mary's Crime

The case for the prosecution wasted no time in painting Mary as a cold blooded killer, who left her husband to die without remorse. Admittedly, the plain facts of the case made Mary seem unbelievably guilty. The prosecution relied on several of these facts in their attempt to convince the jury of Mary's guilt for the charge of murder.

Mary had disconnected the phone immediately after she shot her husband, stopping him from being able to call the emergency services, or receive any calls that may have come in. This suggested that Mary had been in full control of her actions, not panicking, since it is unlikely that somebody in a state of anxiety would think to disconnect the phone.

The fact that Mary had attempted to flee to Orange Beach, Alabama, was also a key point for the prosecution. Immediately after Matthew's death, Mary had taken the family minivan to the beach, with her three children. Later on in her defence, Mary would claim that she ran because '[n]obody would believe me, and they'd take the girls away and put me away.' Certainly, in many murder cases, the fact that the defendant flees the scene is a certain indicator of guilt.

The family's daughter Patricia testified that she couldn't understand her mother's actions. All that she knew was that she had heard a 'big boom', and the sound of something heavy hitting the floor. She quickly ran to the bedroom to see her father on the floor, and her mother holding the shotgun. She had no idea what could possibly have provoked her mother to shoot him.

Another sticking point was that the family finances had been 'in shambles' just before the murder had taken place. This had led Mary to become embroiled in what is called a 'check kiting' scam. In it, she had received checks from unidentified accounts in Canada and Nigeria, and had ultimately fallen to a financial scam that had lost the family money. Prosecutors claimed that this could have somehow instigated the argument that led to Matthew's death, and that Mary had felt as if she had no way out of the scam.

They also jumped on the fact that in an initial conversation with investigators, Mary had told them that their marriage was a happy one, and that '[t]here's no poor me. I'm in control.' They clearly wanted to paint a picture of Mary as remorseless, deceitful, and smarter than she looked.

The Cross-examination

During her cross-examination in court, Mary stated that she didn't remember grabbing the gun from the closet in which it was kept. What she did remember was that 'something went off', 'hearing a loud boom', and that 'it wasn't as loud as I thought it would be.' She did admit that she had shot her husband. Matthew rolled from the bed- upon which he had been lying as they had argued- and dropped to the floor. Mary described smelling gunpowder.

Prosecutor Walter Freeland asked her whether she understood that 'pulling a trigger is what makes it go boom', to which she replied that she did.

Matthew asked her why she had snapped and shot him. She could only say 'I'm sorry.' The shotgun blast had been inflicted from behind, directly into Matthew's back, and had caused severe damage to his organs and spine. According to prosecutors, he had in fact still been alive as Mary had run from the house.

But these simple facts were far from the end of the story, as Mary was to reveal.

Appearances and Revelations

At first, Mary spoke of her husband not in the past tense, but in the present, as if she couldn't quite understand how final her actions really had been. In reminiscing about happier times, Mary told the court that her husband was an intelligent, social man, and that the family had shared many 'good times' together. She also seemed to enjoy talking about her children, and the happiness they brought her.

This happy family life, however, was simply one side of the marriage. Mary's attorney stated that '[w]hat went on behind their closed doors is going to have to be told ... Some of what we've got from the state of Tennessee touches on sexual abuse.' Their defence was that Matthew had made Mary's life a 'living hell': '[w]e will show you proof that he would destroy objects that she loved, he would isolate her from her family and he would abuse her not just verbally, not just emotional and not just physically—in other ways, too.'

Just before the murder, Mary claimed that Matthew had been threatening their children and even attempted to throttle their infant daughter, Breanna. He had been shouting, angry, because he had wanted a son. As the case went on, it became obvious that this was only the tip of the iceberg, however, and more and more sordid details of their home life would come to light.

Matthew, Mary claimed, was a violent, abusive husband. Shortly after their marriage, he ordered her to stop socialising with any of her family and friends (a common tactic among abusive spouses in order to further isolate their partners from potential help). Winkler's sisters described how Mary seemed stuck in her marriage, unhappy, but unable to leave. In an interview, they said that 'As the years went on, she seemed to be nervous to show love towards us.'

Mary was commonly 'screamed and hollered' at by her husband. 'He just flailed. He's a big guy and he was just all over ... He'd point his finger inches away from my nose. Whatever he was upset about, it was my fault,' Mary had said. It could be over anything: 'I was fat, my hair wasn't right, the girls, if something went wrong, it was my fault. I didn't know when it was coming.' Mary described her situation as one familiar to abused wives and husbands across America.

Her attorney, Steve Farese, provided further information based on his conversations with Mary. She had needed her husband's permission for everything, even for getting her hair cut. 'This was constant, and she lived a life where she walked on eggshells.' This abuse, he said, had given Mary symptoms of post traumatic stress disorder, simply because 'she didn't know what was going to happen next.' Furthermore, a psychologist testified as part of Mary's defence, saying that her symptoms were those of clinical depression and PTSD.

During her time on the stand, Mary also claimed that Matthew had forced her to watch pornography with him, and that he had bought her several 'slutty' costumes for sex, which she normally would never have worn, but for fear of her husband. If she refused, Matthew wouldn't hesitate to get physical, hitting her or even using his belt to whip her. Mary famously produced a wig and a pair of white high heels in the witness box during her cross-examination to show the court evidence of Matthew's other side.

Mary stated that she was never happy watching pornography, dressing up in sexy outfits or performing the sex acts that Matthew wanted. She went along with his ideas, however, because she didn't dare face his reaction if she didn't. 'I'd just do anything to help him stay happy.' Throughout these revelations, Mary was visibly embarrassed and uncomfortable. Clearly she would have preferred that none of them had ever come to light; but Mary felt it necessary to brave what her neighbors, and the nation, might think in order to clear her name and justify her actions.

Mary's family had been quick to corroborate her side of the story. Her father, Clark Freeman, had spoken out through Good Morning America and detailed the 'physical, mental, verbal' abuse that his daughter had suffered. Other friends came forward during the court case, and gave similar verdicts on their relationship. A friend of Mary's,

Rudie Thomsen, said that '[o]ne Sunday, Mary came into the church and I looked at her and she had a black eye.' Similarly, Mary's friend Amy Redmon agreed that Matthew had been controlling: '[h]e was an authority figure, and he made the decisions basically. It was obvious.'

Conversely, Matthew's family denied that their son had been anything like Mary had depicted in her defence testimony. Matthew's father, Charles Daniel Winkler, said that his son was a kind, gentle man, who could have done nothing to justify what the defence was claiming. Diane spoke several times during the trial, lashing out at Mary: 'You've never told your girls you're sorry! Don't you think you at least owe them that?'

The dramatic story of a supposedly kindly, gentle church minister having such a sordid, cruel and abusive hidden life gripped America. The case was covered extensively on all major networks, discussed on late night panel shows

The Jury's Verdict

While the prosecutors had tried to convince the jury to convict her on a charge of first degree murder, they were unsuccessful. The jury came to their verdict by April, that year. It took them eight hours to deliberate their way to the decision; this mirrored the response of the nation, which was similarly undecided on just what punishment Mary really deserved.

Mary was found guilty of voluntary manslaughter, a charge which carries a far more lenient sentence than murder. While murderers can receive full life sentences, and in certain states receive the death penalty, the maximum sentence for voluntary manslaughter is only 6 years.

Mary showed little emotion at the verdict, but did embrace each of her relatives afterwards. In a show of support, her family had been sat in the row behind her, and all linked arms with one another to demonstrate their solidarity. Afterwards, she was taken back into custody to await sentencing.

Mary's attorney stated afterwards that Mary's testimony had been central in securing the more lenient sentence. 'I think Mary's testimony was integral in this decision. They had to hear it from Mary', Farese told the press. 'They judged her credibility and they saw that she had an abusive relationship and they made their judgment based upon that.'

For Mary, the most important implication of the verdict was that she could finally begin to think of being reunited with her children. Speaking on her behalf after the trial, Farese continued: 'We would like to do so many things to open up communication between Mary and the paternal grandparents and to get the children out of this cycle of constant upheaval over this terrible tragic event.' But the question of how long she would be in prison remained.

Mary's sentencing was scheduled for May 18th, at which point both Mary and the prosecution would have a final chance to address the court before the judge decided on the final jail term. However, the situation looked positive for Mary. Not only would the five months that she had been imprisoned awaiting trial be taken into consideration, but the judge had indicated that alternatives to incarceration would be on the table. Perhaps Mary could avoid jail time altogether.

Sentencing: The Trial at an End

Due to a scheduling error, the hearing took place around three weeks late, on June 8th.

Mary took to the stand one last time to plead for mercy. She read aloud from a prepared statement, telling Matthew's family of her sorrow and remorse for her actions. She was 'so sorry that this had happened', and would 'always miss and love' her husband. 'I ask for mercy and understanding, but I know whatever decision you reach today will be right ... I ask you to please let me go home today and be with my children.' Tabitha Freeman- Mary's sister- had also pleaded for leniency, in particular to let Mary be reunited with her children. She went as far as calling Mary 'the best example of a good person I can think of'.

Members of Matthew's family, too, took to the stand to plead their case for the prosecution. Charles and his wife were clearly hurt and in disbelief at Mary's actions both in murdering their son, and believed that Mary had purposefully smeared his name at trial. 'The monster that you have painted for the world to see? I don't think that monster existed,' Diane Winkler had said.

After speaking their pieces, all that Mary, her family, and Matthew's parents could do was wait until the judge's decision. The trial- as well as the very public 'trial' that Mary had been through in the media- was finally at an end.

The defence had requested that Mary be granted full probation, or judicial diversion, both outcomes which would have meant that Mary would spent no further time in prison, and even that her record would be cleared of wrongdoing altogether. This request was denied.

After recess, Mary was told that she would spend 3 years in prison for her crime. But Circuit Judge J. Weber McCraw reduced that amount to just 210 days total in prison before she would be allowed to leave on probation. She also had that sentence reduced further, due to the fact that she had spent five months incarcerated waiting for trial.

Moreover, that time would be spent not in jail, but in a mental health centre in Tennessee. There, she would receive treatment for both her depression and post traumatic stress disorder. After such a long ordeal, with the prosecution fighting to either put Mary on death row or to imprison her indefinitely, it seemed that she had gotten off with hardly a slap on the wrist.

Steve Farese branded the sentence 'a victory': '[s]he could be in prison for life, and that's what everybody thought she was headed for to begin with.' Her other attorney, Leslie Ballin, said '[s]he'll be able to get out and fight the battle she wants to, and that is to get her children back.' Mary could finally think about the future again.

But certain signs indicated that it would not be as easy to reconcile with her children and family as she might hope. Matthew's family left the courtroom without making a comment to the press, as did the prosecution, clearly disappointed in the verdict. They gave no indication that they would be happy to open dialogue about Mary's daughters- not with the woman whom they believed to have murdered their son in cold blood.

The aftermath of Mary's release

Mary was released on August 14th, 2007. She had only been sentenced the previous June.

Upon her release, her lawyer informed the press that Mary would not be speaking with them, to maintain her privacy. During her time in the mental health facility, Mary could finally begin her attempt to win full custody of her three daughters, and she was still fighting this case at the time of her release. She had not seen her children, apart from Patricia's brief testimony as part of the case, for over a year. Throughout the case, and after Mary's release, her children were staying with Matthew's family.

Moreover, she was still fighting a $2 million dollar civil lawsuit filed by Matthew's parents. They also took legal measures, which, if successful, would have meant that the custody of Mary's children remained with them.

After her release, Mary seemed happier to her family and friends. From an outside perspective, it could be easy to claim that this was just as much due to her happiness at avoiding a jail sentence as it was to her being rid of an abuser. She was in fact living with friends at first after her release, and went back to work at a dry cleaners in McMinnville, Tenn., 200 miles from Selmer.

In the same interview as was mentioned before, Mary's sisters agreed that she had changed entirely. After years of shyness, Mary seeming unable or unwilling to show love to them for fear of her husband's violence, she seemed to finally be able to open up. 'Now it's back to the old Mary [who] loves us and doesn't care to come and hug us and gives us a kiss on the cheek.'

Since then, Mary lived in McMinnville. She has moved between jobs, working at the dry cleaners, before starting work at a nursery. She briefly dated the brother of one of her most vocal supporters, Paul Pillow; afterwards, she moved in with Wayne Cantrell, a preacher living in Smithville nearby.

Mary regained custody of her three children in 2008, but by 2010, received the news that she had multiple sclerosis. Her diagnosis came at the worst time, as she was settling down in her new life; she had not long started medical school with the desire to become a nurse, and had to quit since the work would be too demanding. She hasn't returned to work since.

One comfort for Mary was that Matthew's parents seemed close to being able to forgive her. After her diagnosis, they gave Mary some time off from parenting by taking care of the children for a weekend, which soon turned into several months. Daniel Winkler has preached several times since the events on the topic of forgiveness, although when asked by local press why he chose the topic, he has refused to answer, presumably preferring to keep those details private.

Mary, too, preferred to put the past behind her. In an interview with WAFF 48, the NBC affiliate in Huntsville AL., she stated how she would prefer to stay out of the limelight, particularly for the sake of her girls. 'Whatever reason people have any problem with me, that's fine. Everybody's entitled to their opinion, but these girls are treated for who they are, not because of what their mother's done ... They're three very fine young ladies'.

Concluding Thoughts

Some members of the public reacted with disgust at the abnormally short sentence that Mary was given, and questioned whether a husband would have been given the same leniency as Mary was. Men's rights activist Glenn Sacks publicly questioned whether a man would have been shown such leniency, and pointed to the case of Scott Peterson (who received the death penalty for the murder of his pregnant wife) to indicate that no, a man would not. He also argued that the idea of abuse had been widened to include simple criticism, and should therefore not necessarily be used as defence of murder.

Conversely, there have been many women put in prison for murdering their abusive husbands, some for much longer than Mary Winkler. The 'battered woman defense', or the preferred terminology today of 'battering and its effects', is not a genuine legal defence in itself; it can, however, be used to convince a court of diminished responsibility. Its effectiveness is due to the sympathy that it elicits from jurors, who can be convinced that abuse is a form of provocation, and the murder a form of self defense. Under this defense, Mary's short sentence makes sense.

The case has remained a touch stone with regards to spousal abuse in the U.S. A made-for-TV movie, 'The Pastor's Wife', was released in 2011. It was based on the book of the same title, written by Dianne Fanning, an award winning crime writer. The story was changed somewhat, with the inclusion of a financial subplot involving tax fraud. However, it also made use of real life interviews with people who knew the Winklers- including Matthew's parents. His mother revealed that she could never believe Mary's story. Charles admitted that Mary's story could be true, and that he could forgive her if she confessed her purposeful intention to murder Matthew.

As for the community in which the family had lived, the reaction was largely one of forgiveness. According to members of that community, the town's 'Christian roots and ... its tendency to give people the benefit of the doubt' meant that they took Mary at her word. Mary's quite life in McMinnville and Smithville similarly shows that the American public would rather leave her and her family alone after their painful ordeal.